pĭ-kyo͞ol´-yər
pi-'kyül-y&r
pih **kyul** yEr

uncommon, unusual, choice, different from the usual or normal, distinctive, pure, holy, set apart

PECULIAR
IN A GOOD WAY

MARY ELLEN EDMUNDS

SALT LAKE CITY, UTAH

My deepest appreciation to the Arrowheads:

Ann, Anne, Barbara, Carolyn,

Debbie, Dorothy, Jane, Leanne,

Lori, Nancy, and Robin

Visit us at deseretbook.com.

Library of Congress Cataloging-in-Publication Data

Edmunds, Mary Ellen, 1940-

Peculiar—in a good way / Mary Ellen Edmunds.

p. cm.

ISBN-13: 978-1-59038-663-7 (pbk.)

ISBN-10: 1-59038-663-9 (pbk.)

1. Mormon women—Religious life. I. Title.

BX8641.E36 2006

248.8'43088289332—dc22 2006016048

Printed in the United States of America

Publishers Printing, Salt Lake City, Utah

10 9 8 7 6 5 4 3 2 1

Contents

Preface

I'm so glad you picked up this peculiar little book. (It started out HUGE, but I just kept chopping away. I didn't want it to weigh eighteen pounds or something.) I know there are a lot of books on store shelves about a variety of topics that may grab more attention than this one about being peculiar. But if you've chosen to read this one, welcome! I sincerely hope your reading and pondering experience will be enjoyable and meaningful.

I hope you have chosen to read this little book because you love and want to learn, and you're looking for some ideas on how to be a happy, obedient, genuine child of God. I write of the possibility of being peculiar among the peculiar. Look at the flowers on the cover. They're all in the same "flower family," but one is standing out.

We stand out when we're a lily among roses, or a cactus

among palms, but we can also stand out—be unusual, uncommon—when we're a daisy with other daisies. I'm hoping in this book I have explained what I mean by our striving to be better when we're already pretty good. That's one of the main themes.

I know I'm going to use that word *peculiar* WAY too much . . . get over it! Ha ha. I just love it that our Heavenly Father wants us to be peculiar, so it has come to be a very positive word for me.

One thing I want to admit is that I decided about midway through working on this book that I wanted to use CAPS for emphasis rather than the customary italics. My editor asked me why. I don't know. I LIKE caps. Maybe it comes from a lifetime of writing notes in capital letters. Anyway, I use quite a few caps, which likely will make the book a little bit more peculiar than it already was.

At the end of some of the chapters I have listed books or articles under the heading "Highly Recommended Reading." These suggestions aren't meant to include all the wonderful material there is on any topic I've touched on, but once in a while I couldn't help myself—there was something I had read that seemed so good, I just had to share! Obviously, I'd recommend that you add your own references to these lists. Someday when you see me, let me know about your favorites.

I am so grateful to the folks at Deseret Book who give such wonderful help. Jana Erickson, Emily Watts, Sheryl Dickert Smith, and Tonya Facemyer all shared their expertise to create the book you hold in your hands. Without the help, encouragement, and patience (yea, even long-suffering at times!) this great Deseret Book team has had for me, I might never have finished.

For each book sold, I will donate to a wonderful organization called CARE FOR LIFE. This foundation was created by Blair and Cindy Packard of Gilbert, Arizona. Go to their web site to learn more: www.careforlife.org

Cindy and Blair are wonderfully peculiar people doing wonderfully uncommon things in the African country of Mozambique, and by the time you read this book they will be President and Sister Packard—mission president and companion. (Or they may have returned home from Mozambique if it's a while before you read this; we don't want to leave them there TOO long!)

Thanks for helping!

CHAPTER 1

On Being Peculiar

I, MEE, having been born of peculiar parents . . .

What comes to your mind when you hear the word *peculiar*? Some think of other words like *strange, odd,* or *weird.* But there's more to the word than that, isn't there?

One dictionary explains that the word *peculiar* means: "That which pertains to or characterizes an individual person, place or thing, or group of persons or things, as distinct from others. *Set apart.* [Really! That definition is in several dictionaries!] Distinguished in nature, character, or attributes from others. Unlike others, singular, uncommon, unusual" (*The New Shorter Oxford English Dictionary,* Oxford: Clarendon Press, 1993; emphasis added).

What are some things that make us—both as a people and as individuals—distinct, uncommon, set apart? It's not the horns, is it? Do you know that there are still people who ask about that: "Do Mormons have horns?" Well, yes, but we keep them well hidden. Some of us keep them in a safety deposit box or under a stunning wig.

In this book I'd love to explore with you the notion of being peculiar people. I don't want to add a lot of unnecessary pressure, guilt, or frustration to your life—I've consciously tried not to do that. What I hope to do is invite you to consider the joys of being increasingly distinct and different in good ways, holy ways, Christlike and Godlike ways.

One of the important phrases that keeps popping up as I've been working on the book is "striving to be better when you're already pretty good." I love that phrase! I hope it will be on your mind as you read, because I'm guessing that we're all probably pretty good, but that something in our hearts and souls wants us to be even better.

So, going back to the opening line of this chapter, what made my parents peculiar? Everything, really. I'm convinced that these two people, Paul K Edmunds and Ella Mary Middleton, were chosen to bring me to this part of my existence, to teach and nurture and endure me.

When I tell others about my parents, I sometimes start by saying my dad was a doctor and my mother a nurse. That is, after all, how they met. They were the only two single, LDS, medical staff people at the hospital in Hanford, California, in about 1936.

My parents were definitely peculiar, and I even have four peculiar brothers and three peculiar sisters! Imagine eight very different children born to the same parents. To be honest, I might be one of the most peculiar of the eight.

Isn't it fascinating how a whole lot of people can all live in the same home, have the same parents (or parent), eat approximately the same things, have similar experiences, and yet turn out to be so DIFFERENT from each other?

As I think of my childhood, I am amazed that our parents were able to allow each of the eight of us children to find our unique personalities, our brought-it-with-us interests and talents. I've often said that Charlotte's dolls went to dances and my dolls went to war. How is it that our parents allowed these differences, even if they had hoped I would be more like Charlotte? (Interestingly, as the years have gone by, I've had lots of times when I'VE wished I could be more like her!)

Thinking about my parents and my family, I look back at that first verse in the Book of Mormon again. I have thought a lot about what Nephi said in that one verse concerning his life, and about how his experiences compared with mine.

My parents weren't asked to take the eight of us into the wilderness, and obviously they didn't send my brothers back to our hometown to find me a husband.

But my peculiar parents were good(ly), and I was taught a lot by both of them. They both used to read to us children when we were little, and they always encouraged us to study hard, speak well, live the Golden Rule, and develop good manners.

Nephi talked of his afflictions, and although I used to think that my older brother was trying to kill me, I know he wasn't really. Compared to what Nephi went through, I can't say honestly that I've seen MANY afflictions in the course of my days. Quite a few, but not MANY. Mine don't come at all close to Nephi's in quality OR quantity.

I do feel like I've been highly favored of the Lord. He has been so generous and kind to me, and has blessed me abundantly all my days. I have felt and continue to feel His goodness.

And if the "mysteries of God" are things like how nine pennies go further than ten, and how nine minutes go further than ten, then I've had some great knowledge of those.

Unlike Nephi and my own father, I haven't been great at keeping a record of my proceedings all my days. I've both lived and recorded some of my days and years better than others.

Nephi's righteousness stood out in comparison to his brothers' bad behavior, but I find myself wondering, what if everyone in his family had been a believer? Is it possible to be peculiar among the peculiar—a light among lights, an example among examples? I'm asking if there are different levels or depths of devotion, obedience, passion, commitment . . . and I'm thinking it IS possible to be peculiar among the peculiar.

Sometimes, when I teach a group of young people, I ask how many are the only LDS student in their school, or one of the very few LDS students. Then I ask them what it's like, if it's difficult, and what their example means to others. I've had some fantastic responses.

But I've also thought and asked about what it's like to be LDS in a mostly LDS school or workplace or neighborhood. Can a light shine brightly there too?

Maybe you're the only one in your family to have joined the Church. That brings some changes and differences, doesn't it?

Or maybe you were raised in an LDS home and yet have realized that there are different levels of commitment—conversion—among your family members. There may have been times when even your closest loved ones have not seemed to understand your behavior, your devotion.

As an example, perhaps you have developed a different feeling about how to keep the Sabbath day holy from that of others in your family. You may have experienced the sting of having others call you "goody-two-shoes" (whatever that means) or some other unkind thing. Maybe you've been "accused" of being overly religious. Maybe you've been told that you're taking things way too seriously. I've wondered if such criticism, such judging, hurts more when it comes from family members than from others.

Maybe your heart aches for loved ones, including family or friends, who seem to have decided that other things are more important than being true and faithful.

On the other hand, maybe there's some Super Saint in your family or neighborhood or ward who can't believe you're not yet sprouting wheat and making your own clothes. And where is your compost pile? (Or: "What? You've never quilted!?")

Maybe you feel the way I do sometimes—like a struggling pilgrim who realizes that it's not helpful to have others point out ways in which you're not yet perfect. We all could probably use more encouragement and less judging.

Most of us have had experiences where friends knew of our

standards and either made fun of them or showed respect. I think it's probable that our example has been more of a positive influence on others than we realize.

Let me illustrate by sharing something that happened when I was about eighteen and my younger sister Susan was twelve. She'd been invited to a slumber party at a friend's home, but she called me at around 10:00 P.M. asking if I would come to get her. I could tell she was trying not to let me know she was crying. I asked what the problem was, and she said some of the other girls were swearing.

This may seem like a tiny thing, but she had decided she didn't want to swear, and it upset her that those who attended the same Primary classes she did and heard the same talks and read the same scripture verses were making different choices. She was hurt and disappointed.

I felt proud of her for not following the others, for being willing to stand alone.

I talked to her for a while, and she decided to stay at the party and ask her friends to please stop swearing. When Charlotte and I went to pick her up the next morning, she was a happy girl. Things had improved, and she'd had a good time.

What would it be like if we could be depended upon to live what we believe, what we've been taught? Imagine the difference we could make in the world, starting in our own homes and neighborhoods and villages! The power of a good example is hard to measure adequately.

It would be wonderful if there were a "generic resume" that could apply to all Latter-day Saints. It could include things like:

She is absolutely honest.

She does not smoke, drink, or do drugs.

She will give an honest day's work for an honest day's wage.

She has been taught the work ethic, and she's a hard worker.

You will find her to be cheerful, optimistic, and positive.

You can trust her.

And then we could just add to it our particular preparation, skills, education, and experience: "Cabin Maid at Zion National Park." "Salesman for *Humpty Dumpty* magazine for one year." Whatever.

Wouldn't it be something if we all did our best to live what we believe in such a way that others would become increasingly aware of qualities they could count on in Latter-day Saints?

Elder J. Richard Clarke illustrated what I'm trying to say by sharing an experience he had years ago while attending general conference. He went to purchase some things at ZCMI and needed to cash a check. Since he was from out of state, the cashier asked for some ID. Elder Clarke reached in his wallet to get some credit cards, and his temple recommend came out. As he tells it:

> The cashier said, "I'll accept that." I said, "You'll accept what?" She said, "Your temple recommend. It's current, isn't it?" I said, "Yes, it's current." She said, "That will do."

Elder Clarke said he pondered this all the way home.

> I thought, Wouldn't it be a great idea if we had a Mormon credit card? A card-carrying Mormon could

> be depended on to keep his word, to be honest with his employers, and to pay his bills as agreed. . . .
>
> Wouldn't it be wonderful to be a "peculiar" people known for our honesty and the quality of our services? The Mormon standard of integrity should be the highest standard in all the world, for we are the covenant people of God. The Lord makes no special concessions for culture, race, or nationality; He expects all His Saints to live according to gospel standards ("The Practice of Truth," *Ensign*, May 1984, 62–63).

There is a difference between living the gospel and merely participating in church meetings and activities, isn't there? Church meetings and activities, and even some church assignments, come to an end when we hear an "Amen." But living the gospel is something for every inch and minute of our lives—for every step we take, every word we say, every thought we think. It's like an invitation put this way: "Every member a member!"

I can remember times when I've noticed someone wearing a CTR ring, a Young Women medallion, an Eagle Scout pin, or I can tell they've been to the temple, and I've felt like I was near someone I could trust. Once when my brother and his children were driving to California, they stopped to help someone stranded by the side of the road. Later, the children said they'd been a bit worried until they saw "the smile showing through his T-shirt."

Perhaps someone is carrying or reading scriptures or an *Ensign* or a book you recognize as being a good one.

Maybe you're at the beach and you see a family or group in which everyone is dressed modestly, and you wonder, "RULDS2?" (I know that's on a license plate somewhere.)

Maybe it's Monday evening, and you see a family bowling, playing miniature golf, or going to a movie together. Maybe they're singing "Popcorn Popping on the Apricot Tree" in their car.

There are lots of ways to recognize other "peculiar people," aren't there? Oh, if we could consistently trust and be trusted!

There are many scriptural references that help explain our uniqueness as covenant Saints, and why we do what we do. Join with me in a little review.

Exodus 19:5: "Now therefore, if ye will obey my voice indeed, and keep my covenant, then ye shall be a peculiar treasure unto me above all people: for all the earth is mine." (Sometimes when I read and think about that one I make a tiny little adjustment: "if ye will obey my voice IN DEED," meaning to me that we obey by doing, especially by our good deeds.)

Deuteronomy 26:18: "And the Lord hath avouched thee [I don't think it hurts to be avouched] this day to be his peculiar people, as he hath promised thee, and that thou shouldest keep all his commandments."

I became interested in that word *avouched,* and was carried away happily for a little while looking up meanings. Elder Bruce R. McConkie used it in a conference talk in a way that helped me understand it better:

> We glory in our designation as a peculiar people. It is our desire to be unique—different from other

> men—because we have forsaken the world and have made a covenant to live godly lives and to walk in paths of truth and virtue.
>
> It is our hope that it may ever be said of us, as Peter avouched of the true believers in his day: "Ye are a chosen generation, a royal priesthood, an holy nation, a peculiar people. . . ." (1 Pet. 2:9) ("The Mystery of Mormonism," *Ensign*, November 1979, 53–54).

The word *avouched,* then, seems to imply an affirmation, something that is declared or witnessed or testified of. Now, with that definition and description in mind, read with me from Deuteronomy 26:17–19 again:

> Thou hast avouched the Lord this day to be thy God, and to walk in his ways, and to keep his statutes, and his commandments, and his judgments, and to hearken unto his voice:
>
> And the Lord hath avouched thee this day to be his peculiar people, as he hath promised thee, and that thou shouldest keep all his commandments;
>
> And to make thee high above all nations which he hath made, in praise, and in name, and in honour; and that thou mayest be an holy people unto the Lord thy God, as he hath spoken.

"Thou hast avouched the Lord this day to be thy God!" Yes! And He has avouched us as we seek to keep our covenants, to become better increasingly through our choices and His gentle help, and to serve others.

All this avouching is a good thing!

For this chapter I chose the title "On Being Peculiar" because it seems to me that we all have an invitation from God to become choice, favored, pure, chosen, unusual, uncommon, singular, extraordinary . . . peculiar. It's a call from a Heavenly Father to His children to become as He is.

John Tanner put it this way: "Peculiar literally means we are his special treasure, purchased with his blood" ("To Clothe a Temple," *Ensign*, August 1992, 47). Why were we purchased at such a great cost? Why does our Heavenly Father ask us to be "an holy nation, a peculiar people" (1 Peter 2:9)?

One reason that came to me was that it is for our safety and protection. We're never asked to do anything stupid—but we *are* asked to do and be that which will qualify us to return Home to our Heavenly Parents kind and dear, to be with Them and our other loved ones forever.

Another reason we are asked to be holy and set apart is because we can't DO good unless we ARE good. I keep remembering that "A good tree cannot bring forth evil fruit, neither can a corrupt tree bring forth good fruit" (Matthew 7:18).

And we are asked to be peculiar so that we can be a light to others. We are asked to be examples—to be there so others can lean on us if they become confused, weak, discouraged, lonely, overwhelmed, or lost. We can and do become a safe place, a refuge from the storm.

President Spencer W. Kimball spoke clearly of the power of

our example at the general women's meeting on September 15, 1979:

> Much of the major growth that is coming to the Church in the last days will come because many of the good women of the world (in whom there is often such an inner sense of spirituality) will be drawn to the Church in large numbers. This will happen to the degree that the women of the Church reflect righteousness and articulateness in their lives and to the degree that the women of the Church are seen as distinct and different—in happy ways—from the women of the world. . . .
>
> Thus it will be that female exemplars of the Church will be a significant force in both the numerical and the spiritual growth of the Church in the last days.
>
> No wonder the adversary strives, even now, to prevent this from happening! ("The Role of Righteous Women," *Ensign*, November 1979, 103–4).

Distinct and different in HAPPY WAYS from the women of the world. That is such an attractive idea, isn't it? It implies optimism, a perfect brightness of hope, being positive and upbeat. And of course the words *distinct* and *different* are synonyms of *peculiar.*

Recently I landed at the airport in Long Beach early in the morning and had a bit of a wait before my friend came to pick me up. I was sitting on an outside bench by a woman who was also waiting, and I struck up a conversation with her.

She was from Sweden, and since I'd had the chance to travel there a couple of years earlier, I could comment on how beautiful it was. She asked how I came to go there, and I asked her if she had ever seen the LDS temple there. She said yes. I told her that my sister and her husband had served in that temple, and I had gone to see them.

She asked if they were missionaries, and then said, "I'm LDS too." Instantly we had so much more to share! We both remarked on how we can find sisters and brothers—friends—everywhere we go.

And then we were saying that if we were to whistle or hum a hymn almost anywhere in the world, someone would likely hear and respond.

One summer when I was working as a camp nurse at Shady Lawn Farm in Oakdale, California, I was helping my sister Susan, who was employed to teach children to ride horses, with an evening devotional. At the end of her short presentation, she asked me to sing "O My Father" with her.

As we began singing, two other campers came running to join us. We hadn't known they were LDS, but the hymn was a magnet, and they finished singing with us and became our dear friends.

So sometimes being peculiar sets us apart from others, and many times it brings us together.

One other memory of the camp is when our youngest brother, Richard, went with us to Shady Lawn Farm when he was ten. We loved watching him at mealtime. The way the camp leaders had us express thanks for our food was to sing "Johnny Appleseed," which begins, "Oh the Lord is good to me, and so I thank the Lord . . ." Susan and I would notice with emotion and joy that after this, at each meal, Richard would bow his head and do the "I've got something in my eye" thing (rubbing his eyes until he had finished his own little prayer). His peculiar upbringing showed itself even at that tender age.

I like to tell people that our peculiar family never, ever watched TV on Sunday during my growing-up years. We never even turned on the TV on Sundays!

Then, of course, I have to admit that we didn't HAVE a TV, and with that revelation I'm admitting that we weren't perfect at all. But we WERE trying to progress toward being better.

I want to make sure that struggling pilgrims like MEE don't turn away from this book, thinking it's just for those who are only a few inches and breaths away from perfection. These are the things I'M working on. I've worked hard to not soften the message but to admit and illustrate that the whole idea is to start where we are and press forward, upward, the best we can.

I've wanted to make it a positive book, not one that makes anyone feel like they're not doing enough or being enough. And yet I couldn't resist the notion of striving to be better when we're already pretty good. I couldn't take out of my mind the Lord's invitation to "be ye therefore perfect" (Matthew 5:48).

Did you choose to read this little book because you want to find some ideas about how to apply the gospel in a way that brings more happiness every day? Are you interested in striving to become increasingly true and faithful? Would you like to consider some ways to become more genuine?

As we work toward these goals, we need to ponder the difference between wanting to be righteous and sliding into hypocrisy, pretense, and self-righteousness. We're NOT striving to be better so we can feel superior, or so we can always be right or always "win."

Is that a danger? "Here I am rising toward heaven, while all around me the masses are full of iniquity, being dragged carefully down to . . ."

Oh, that is so *opposite* of what I want to emphasize and encourage!

I almost feel that as we genuinely strive to be more holy, more Godlike and Christlike, we recognize more clearly our weaknesses, and we plead for mercy and Heavenly help. That's much different from the "holier-than-thou" kind of attitude that looks down at the masses from its personal Rameumpton. YUK!

Remember that, as Elder Dallin H. Oaks has taught, our strengths can become our downfalls.

It is so much better for others when we stand ready to support them in making changes rather than constantly judging. We struggle with different challenges, but kindness can help more than we may recognize. I hope that you will feel encouraged to be the best YOU possible, and to help others be their own best too.

So, is there any little or medium or even big thing you could do differently today? Is there some change you could make that wouldn't ruin your whole schedule and cut too deeply into laundry time?

Could you eat just one bite of the Big Elephant today? Even just ten or fifteen minutes' worth?

I hope in your reading and thinking (and you certainly don't have to read this whole book in a hurry) you'll mostly find out that you're doing a LOT of wonderful things without realizing that they "counted." Do you know what I mean?

Many speakers and writers put it this way: "You're better than you think you are." I'm convinced that's true for everyone I've ever met.

Recently I was visiting with a woman who was struggling with her level of self-worth (it had sunk), and I was prompted to say something like, "Oh, my dear friend, I think you are going to be so incredibly surprised someday when you see your Heavenly Father again and realize how deeply He cares for you and how lovingly He'll say, 'Well done!'"

Too often we have a tendency to put ourselves down, to be our worst critics, to fend off any compliments (either from earthlings or from Heaven).

And sometimes we might think that it's a mark of true humility to deflect praise and compliments. I know people who say they have NEVER said to themselves, "Good job!" or "Good for you!"

Wow . . . I can't imagine living a life where you never felt that you had done something you could call good. Ouch. We've got work to do! Changes to make! Possibilities and plans and strategies to consider!

And this whole idea is quite peculiar, isn't it—this desire to be better, and to figure out how to accomplish that.

President Gordon B. Hinckley taught that "If we will live the gospel, if we will put our trust in God, our Eternal Father, if we will do what we are asked to do as members of The Church of Jesus Christ of Latter-day Saints, we will be the happiest and most blessed people on the face of the earth" ("Excerpts from Recent Addresses of President Gordon B. Hinckley," *Ensign*, April 1996, 72).

That's worth some striving, isn't it! Imagine being the happiest and most blessed people on the face of the earth!

Well, wherever we are in our striving, we are children of God, and He loves us. And I feel assured He understands us and blesses our efforts to try hard to do good and to be good.

HIGHLY RECOMMENDED READING

Gerald N. Lund, "I Have a Question," *Ensign*, August 1986, 39–41.

John A. Widtsoe, "I Have a Question: Why are the Latter-day Saints a peculiar people?" *Ensign*, April 1988, 50–51 (originally published in *Improvement Era*, September 1942, 577, 607).

Dallin H. Oaks, "Our Strengths Can Become Our Downfall," *Ensign*, October 1994, 11–19.

CHAPTER 2

What About You and MEE?

You are peculiar. Yes, YOU. Has no one ever pointed that out? Well, it's true.

Understand, of course, that I'm not saying you're weird, odd, or strange. No. I'm saying you're unique. And wonderful and spectacular and amazing. I really am. I have never met anyone who WASN'T unique and interesting!

Perhaps you're taller than most, or shorter. Maybe you have bright red hair or (as in my case) a bright red nose. I like to tell people that when my nose is red it means I'm happy (and I'm happy most of the time).

Maybe something about you caused others to have nicknames for you, some of them fun and some of them awful. Even Rudolph experienced this—we know the other reindeer called him names. That can't have been fun.

I remember hearing a little saying as a child: "Sticks and stones may break my bones, but names will never hurt me." But they DO sometimes, don't they?

You might be someone who once had your hair colored purple or cut in a mohawk. Maybe you even lost all your hair because of chemotherapy, or your sister cut it when your mother wasn't watching.

Did you ever wear anything that took you to the very edge of embarrassment and self-consciousness, but you wore it anyway? Maybe it was something you chose, or maybe it was a hand-me-down that you didn't want to wear.

Once on a dare I wore Bermuda shorts under my nurse's uniform for a whole day. And once at the Missionary Training Center when I wanted to make a statement about how cold my office was, I wore pink, ankle-length long johns under my dress.

I was the first in our town to wear braces, and I can't remember how many times I was asked if I had polio in my teeth. (I got my braces about the time the polio epidemic hit.)

I wore "stand-up-and-shout," heavy, black, corrective shoes for several years. I think the laces were about five feet long . . . but I might be exaggerating a bit, as I'm known to do.

I don't know that I really needed those shoes, but Dad wanted us to have good arches, so on they went. At some point he learned how to tape the arches (probably something he gleaned from watching athletes with their legs taped), and we'd go to school with that attractive addition to our legs, criss-crossed all the way up to our knees.

Dad also had us go barefoot in the house, picking up

marbles with our toes and hauling them around for an "arch exercise."

And whenever we had a scrape or a cut, he would paint us with "purple medicine" (a.k.a. Gentian Violet), so everyone in town knew we were Edmunds children with our purple elbows and knees.

Often I'd do things myself (with no help from Dad) that would draw attention, although that wasn't my specific goal. Like the day I wanted to see what the world *did* look like through rose-colored glasses, so I painted mine. I ended up having to scrape off just a tiny hole through the paint on each lens so I could see to get around. I ended up wondering what all the fuss was about—rose-colored glasses made it harder to see things right in front of me, let alone the world.

Have you ever been in a situation where you were peculiar because you were in the minority? Maybe you were the first female at a previously all-male academy, or maybe you were the first boy to take a home-ec cooking class.

When I lived in Africa, I was definitely in the minority. Sometimes my companion Ann and I would be in the market or in a village—just about anywhere, really—and we'd look around and not see anyone else who looked quite like we did. We used to say the "Three W's" caused us to stand out: White Women Walking. All three were unusual things in our village.

One day, we needed to get our pictures taken for a little identification booklet so that we could be official residents of our village in Nigeria. We heard there was a shop where you could get passport-type photographs taken, so off we went. It took a while, because first the man had to crank up his generator.

After we had smiled brightly and waited many minutes, he showed us the pictures. We burst out laughing—we couldn't help it. All we could see were some slight shadows where our eyes, noses, and lips were. The camera was not set for such washed-out faces; it was set for the beautiful black faces of the Africans.

He tried again, and we got our identification booklets.

It was hard to miss me and my companion Sister Jan Bair as we rode our bikes through the streets of Tainan, Taiwan, in 1962, singing and whistling and enjoying ourselves. It would have been especially hard to miss us on Christmas morning as we rode toward our rented chapel with Santa costumes the Pace family had let us borrow!

I was hard to miss as I jumped in and out of jeepneys and on and off of buses in the Philippines.

And for a year in Solo, Central Java, Indonesia, I didn't see a single other "white woman" riding a bicycle around town. That didn't happen until more sister missionaries came from the USA.

Now it's your turn. Can you remember a time or times when you stood out? What is it about YOU that is uncommon and unusual? What have been your experiences with your unique, interesting self?

Suppose I don't know you but I want to. What would I learn about you if I visited your home? What would I notice? (If you came to visit me, you'd discover that I live right now in a storage shed, but I'm hoping that's about to change as I've worked to give myself more time at home to attack the dust balls and boxes and "stuff.") What's hanging on the walls in your home? What books and magazines do you read? What's circled or underlined in your *TV Guide?*

What would I learn about you if I knew the way you spent your money and your time? What would I learn about you if I listened to how you speak to other people and watched how you treat them?

What would I learn about you from the way you dress? Is there anything "peculiar" about that?

How do you get to know yourself better? I've got some ideas. See if one or more of them would be interesting and helpful to you. Let's start with some questions that might bring things to mind.

Were you (or are you) one of the few LDS students in your school? In your community? In your neighborhood? At work? (I almost put "In your ward?" and maybe that was true too—there may have been just a very few young men or young women.)

Are you exactly like anyone else you know (including brothers and/or sisters)?

How are you different from members of your family?

How are you different from your closest friends?

How are you different now from when you were ten years younger or twenty or thirty? (If you weren't born yet, it may be difficult to answer that, but it might also be very fascinating, eh?)

How would you like to be in ten more years? Twenty? Thirty?

It doesn't take much to get carried away with this kind of thinking. For example, I could start by suggesting that you consider ten family members and observe how you are different and how you are similar.

I would then suggest that you select ten friends and do the same. Then ten people you've never met but have just read about or heard about. Ten fictional characters from books or movies. Ten characters from comic strips (we used to call them the funny papers). Ten animals . . . see what I mean? I was imagining how I'm different from or similar to an elephant, an ant, a baboon, a hippo, an ostrich. Sometimes it's hard to stop when I get on a roll like that!

Now I'd like to suggest some specific activities, and even if you don't choose to do any of them, I hope you'll find them interesting. But come on—just give at least one of them a try and see what you learn about YOU.

1. Think about those who have had a significant influence in your life.

Besides the Savior, your Heavenly Father, and your family, list ten of the most important and influential people in your life. Write the reasons why they are and have been so important to you. Some of these will be people you have known, but some might be people you have only heard of and read about.

Write a letter to each person—even if you don't know how to get it to them. They might be on the Other Side, or they may have moved, or you moved, and you're not sure where they are anymore.

Write a letter anyway. You'll discover and learn a lot.

Here's one of mine:

Dear Helen Keller,

I'm not sure if or when you'll ever read this letter, but I've been wanting to share some things with you for a long time.

When I was twenty-three years old I was in the Philippines as an LDS ("Mormon") missionary (I'm sure you can find someone Up There to explain this to you if you don't already know what it means), and my companion and I had permission to go see a movie about your life called The Miracle Worker. *This movie affected me very deeply. I even suggested to my companion that we stay and watch it again, and she agreed.*

While I'd heard about you in school, I mainly knew that you were deaf and blind, but I had no idea how incredible you are. Were. (Sorry, I don't know if I should use present or past tense, so I hope it doesn't annoy you if I kind of switch back and forth without realizing it.)

After the movie, I couldn't quit thinking about you. I even bought a copy of the book you wrote about your life. And I had dreams about you—you were in the Philippines, and I had the honor of showing you around and answering a lot of your questions.

The reason for my letter is to tell you how much I admire and appreciate you, even though I've never met you. I thank you for your influence on me. I really appreciate the way you've helped me to be more grateful and more aware of blessings.

I can't imagine what it was like for you to be trapped in the dark, and how joyful your life became once "Teacher," Annie Sullivan, came to be with you.

I think both of you are incredible. It's hard for me to imagine that she stayed with you for fifty years! What devotion and friendship!

I look forward to seeing you one of these days. I hope you have found some things that are very precious to me—the gospel of Jesus Christ—and that we can talk about them as well as many, many other things.

Get the idea? Here's just part of another letter I wrote that I never had a chance to send.

Dear Mr. Halversen,

This is a letter that is long overdue. I hope that where you are you can know some of my thoughts, because I guess in a way this is a letter that has been in my heart for many years.

Every so often I have made a list of those who've had the most influence in my life (besides my family), and you, Mr. Halversen, are always in the Top Ten, and often in the Top Five.

I'm not sure if this will surprise you or not. But you really have had a deep and lasting influence on me. I'm so happy we lived on the same street, First West, when I was a little girl. I'm so glad you invited us to see if our parents had a stringed instrument, and that you fixed up my daddy's three-quarter-sized violin and began to teach me how to play.

I can't thank you enough for bringing good music into the life of a little tomboy who had achieved the rank of General at recess. It is hard to calculate fully the difference music has made in my life—the ways in which it has tenderized and thrilled me. I remember getting on my bike to come to my lessons at the Thorley mansion. I had that little wooden case that would come open sometimes, and my violin would bounce out. I'd shove it back in and continue the few blocks to find you waiting patiently.

One thing I loved about my lessons was looking at your hands as you played. I think I'd ask you to repeat something more than I needed, just so I could watch your hands. You were so good! And I loved the way your hands smelled. You probably had some kind of cologne on, and if I were to smell it now it would bring back a million memories.

I loved participating in the Messiah *each year, and it helped me so much when you told me in the beginning (when you had me sit WAY at the back of the orchestra) not to worry about playing all the notes, but just to enjoy the thrill of participating in such a magnificent musical experience.*

Do these excerpts give you an idea about what you might

write? I have to say that once I get going, it's hard to stop! Maybe the same thing will happen to you.

Let someone know how they helped you in your quest to become who you really are. Tell them of some specific ways in which your life is different because of their example and influence.

And here's something you might find just as interesting: Write a letter to *you* from *them*—what would they say to you? Have them tell you what they see in you that is unique and special. Here's a small portion of my "pretend" response from Mr. Halversen:

Dear Mary Ellen,

I was pleasantly surprised to hear from you, and I'm sure you'll be even more surprised to hear from me! It is so natural for me now to realize how close we are that I keep forgetting it's still a mystery to all of you.

I appreciate the kind things you said in your letter. Thank you for taking the time to share. The fact that I'm aware of what you wrote is even more miraculous than email or any other way you have of keeping in touch.

I remember you as an interesting little child. At first I wasn't sure if you could settle down enough to learn to play the violin, but I saw some potential there and rather enjoyed looking forward to a dose of the unexpected each time you came for your lesson.

I remember how hard it was not to be amused when you figured out how to play your violin like a ukulele, and how often I tried to tell you it wasn't appropriate—that your violin was a fine instrument and not a toy.

Do you remember Christmastime in 1954 when I brought some brand-new violins that had been made by Dale Stevens of Salt Lake City? I asked you to choose the one you'd like to play in the Messiah *that year, and you couldn't believe I really meant it.*

You picked my favorite—it not only looked beautiful but it had such a wonderful tone.

You found out after our performance that your parents and I had planned a surprise for you. I remember the look on your face when they came up and said "Merry Christmas," and you realized the violin was their gift to you that year.

Again, that's just a small part of what I wrote.

Okay, I know this won't surprise anyone who knows me, but I kind of got carried away with this and had some fun. I won't include everything, but here's enough of another "exchange" to give you an idea:

Dear Marco Polo,

You'll likely be very surprised to hear from me, as we've never met, but I have been fascinated by your journeys my whole life and have said for years that one thing I'd like to have done is to have gone with you. I would have been so fascinated by the people you met and the lessons you learned.

That's all I'll include of what I wrote to him (even though I know you're dying to hear it all), but now I have to give you a sample of his "response":

Dear Mary Ellen Edmunds,

I don't know how you got my address, but I have NO idea who you are, and NO, I'm not going to be sending you the autographed photo you requested. You're a nervy little earthling, and I'm pretty sure you would have slowed down my traveling, but perhaps we'll meet someday and I'll change my opinion.

You knew I would put something like that in here, didn't you? Couldn't resist! I'm positive Marco Polo would have been much kinder, but I was having fun. I get laughing and playing, and I just can't help myself.

I wanted to contact Eleanor Roosevelt, but she refused my calls. I actually never did meet her, but I thought it would be interesting to get her perspective on what the nation and world were like during my childhood. I had some specific questions about World War II, her husband's mother, Warm Springs, and stuff.

Miss Piggy was on a date.

And all I could get out of Old MacDonald was "EIEIO."

I made other lists, such as ten imaginary friends, and even ten people who could have influenced me but refused to cooperate.

But back to business! Another part of this idea could be to interview people you can still find who knew you at various times in your life. Ask them what was unusual, unique, "peculiar" about you when you were a baby, a child, a teenager, and so on. (You might need courage to do this!)

2. *Pretend you are going to introduce yourself at some event.*

What would you say? How would you introduce yourself?

Or, for a variation of this, write down how another person would introduce you to others in a kind of formal setting. Your best friend. Your boss. Your father or mother. Your child. Your employee. Your bishop. Your neighbor. Your brother or sister. What would they say? How would they introduce you? Why not ask some of them?

I've had a few introductions in my life as I've given talks hither, thither, and yon. (Yes! In all three places!) Some of them have been rather unusual. When I spoke in my friend Nan's stake several years ago, as I remember it, she introduced me as "someone who's had to wear a dress her whole life." Ha. I'd never really thought about it, but it's true.

As a little girl I wore a dress to school every day except "field day," which was one of my favorite days of the year. Even on harsh winter days when we walked to school on snowdrifts, we wore dresses. I'd have my snowsuit pants on underneath, and a warm coat, a hat, boots, and gloves.

This was the case all through high school and college. And while at BYU we even had to wear dresses to athletic events (unless we were participating). Again, no matter what the weather, women wore dresses.

When I became a nurse, we wore dresses: white dresses,

white nylons, white shoes (with Sani-White polish), and white caps (with a black band once we became official RNs).

I've served several missions, where of course I wore dresses.

Then I spent most of my working life in the Missionary Training Center, and I don't need to tell you about the dress code there (*dress* being the operative word in that phrase).

Now, as I watch children on their way to school, it seems more practical to allow some freedom in their clothing, and yet . . .

And when I visit a hospital, it really does seem more practical to have nurses dressed modestly in easy-to-care-for uniforms. And yet . . .

I'm not going to put "and yet" after mentioning wearing comfortable, warm clothing to football games, okay?

Maybe some men wish they still wore hats everywhere, and maybe some women remember with nostalgia what it was like to "dress up" to go downtown.

Shoot, there might be people who wish we still used mimeograph machines or phones with party lines and "number please."

See how that one line from an introduction can get you thinking about your life?

Another introduction I remember was given by my dear friend "Turtle," whose real name was Mary Jane. On one of my visits to Maryland, I'd been asked to give a talk in her stake, and she was asked to introduce me. She gave me this written copy of what she said:

March 1990

I first met Mary Ellen Edmunds in Hong Kong in 1963. In spite of her hilarious letters welcoming me as a missionary to the Southern Far East, I wasn't quite prepared for her. My defenses were down.

When it came time for me to meet my mission president for the first time, I was hiding behind a door barefoot, wondering what to do. Sister Edmunds had tied my shoes to the twenty-foot ceiling of the mission home. I didn't have a clue how to get them down.

I didn't come out until my mission president was really irritated. When I finally did come out, he thundered, "Sister Davidson, WHERE are your shoes!" The next thing I remember him saying was: "Sister Edmunds, see me in my office after dinner." She wasn't scared. She was as much at home with him as she would have been with my little brother. So, that's one side of Sister Edmunds: She plays mean tricks.

Mary Ellen was prepared early in life for such things. One morning, just to see what her reaction would be, her own mother gave her a pie in the face.

Eventually, we were companions in the Philippine Islands for nine months. I got to know her well. I learned she doesn't sleep as much as most people. She kept me up working all night and then made fun of me when I fell asleep on a bus the next day. She said she couldn't decide whether to hold my legs together or to hold my mouth shut to keep me decent in public. Once she tended a little boy all night in a primitive hospital while I slept in the nurses quarters.

There are several things Mary Ellen doesn't like: She can't stand pessimism, she can't stand being late, and she doesn't tolerate dishonesty. I remember a dishonest taxi driver who should have known that before he let her into his cab. Because he guessed we didn't know the territory and was driving us all over town, she grabbed the back of his neck and shook him. He was glad to stop the cab and let us out without paying his outrageous fee.

Mary Ellen has the courage to stand for truth and righteousness under any circumstances. You would want her next to you in a good fight. I have seen her take on a whole gang of ruffians single-handed, just because one of them was harassing me. As a result, she earned the complete admiration of the entire gang. And she was not Gargantua; she was just a slender girl.

Mary Ellen has an elephant-sized heart. That is what drives her to stay up nights, to be a champion of righteousness, and to work with all her might, mind and strength . . . literally. She came home from Africa in a wheelchair.

She loves people. She loves all of us, even though she notices our idiosyncrasies. She is at ease with the famous and the infamous, with the wealthy and the poor, with the suffering and the dying, with the disfigured and the disabled. All of us are safe in her presence (except those who are pessimistic, those who are late, and those who are cheating). Her love is irresistible. It takes away all fear. Everywhere she goes she has a following. She is like the pied piper. Her following includes children and old people, men as well as women, sick and well. I am one of her followers. I love her and consider it a great privilege to be able to introduce her tonight.

I want you to know that I could have edited this, but I left it just the way she wrote it. I'm asking you to take an honest look at yourself in this book, and I figured I should do the same.

And in that spirit I'll share part of an introduction from March 2005. I was in Las Vegas with my friend Leanne, filling in at a women's conference for my friend Sandi who had just had both knees replaced (and we had to laugh because the theme was from Acts 26:16, "Rise, and stand upon thy feet." I'm not kidding! Don't you think that's funny!)

My friend Leanne's introduction on this particular day went on and on, but here are just a few little snippets:

PARKING—Parking is a BIG DEAL and she knows exactly where to park at all of the places she goes to often. For instance, at the Provo Temple in the spring and summer she goes early to get HER parking spot. It is on the far side of the temple on the second row, third space. She goes at the crack of dawn to get this space and she stays for two sessions. When she gets out about 11:00, her car is in the shade. She has similar spots at her chapel, the MTC, the local Wal-Mart, Sam's Club, the post office, etc.

WRITING INSTRUMENTS—Every room in MEE's house has a small box with writing instruments in it. These writing instruments HAVE to be placed in the box in a certain order, all pointing the same direction. Far right is a thin black felt-tip pen, next is a motel-type blue or black ballpoint pen, then a mechanical pencil, then a red felt-tip pen, then a black-ink gel pen, then a thin green pen, then a thicker Sharpie pen. If you should go use one and get them out of order, the next time she went into the room, she would notice and put them right back in order! NO KIDDING.

That's enough for now.

3. Consider writing your last lecture or letter.

I know I've suggested this many times before, but I want to recommend it again. Have you noticed how powerful and tender and poignant some "last lectures" have been? Do you have a last letter from a parent or grandparent or child or friend? Did you find a priceless note when you cleaned a closet or a drawer or went through a box?

See what you learn about yourself by writing a last letter or lecture. Pretend this is your last chance to share some of your deepest feelings. If it helps, address the letter to a specific person, or the lecture to a specific group. And don't let the word *lecture* make it seem too heavy or stuffy.

These may be letters or lectures you will never send or give, but they might become precious to you because of what they teach you about yourself. For me, as I've done this several times, it's become a healing experience.

I hope you'll spend some time with these activities and get to know yourself better. You may even be guided to some things you could do to move forward in your progress.

I'm convinced that the more we strive to become like the Savior, the more peculiar we'll be. We'll notice it, and others likely will too.

HIGHLY RECOMMENDED READING

Anything YOU have written!

CHAPTER 3

Arrows

When I first heard about a program in Scouting called the "Order of the Arrow," I thought it sounded like a wonderful adventure, and I wanted to participate. I enjoyed MIA camp and 4-H and stuff, but I was always curious about what the Scouts got to do for that Order of the Arrow. It seemed like it would be something mysterious, exotic, and challenging.

But it was "SO"—Scouts Only.

So I decided to come up with my own version, and you're all invited to come along! I wish I could offer you a merit badge or something as you complete this activity!

To begin with, draw an arrow on a blank piece of paper (the 8½ x 11-inch size is good for this project, with the paper horizontal). Draw the arrow like the one above, with the "point" on the left and a rather long line going out to the right. (You'll need it longer than it is in the illustration if you get on a roll, and I think you just might get rolling.)

Now you've got your arrow drawn on a good-sized piece of paper, and your pen, brain, and imagination are ready to go. This "homework" could take a little while, but I hope you'll find it meaningful and even fun.

Here's a little story to set the stage. Years ago I was asked to speak at a fireside, and the only person I really knew was the one who had invited me. So I sat quietly and reverently at the back while I waited for her to arrive.

I was sitting behind two older women, and one turned to the other with a question. Her *s*'s whistled as she asked, "Who did you say was speaking this evening?"

Her companion, also whistling her *s*'s a bit, responded, "It's Mary Ellen Edmunds, and I hear she's *very* religious."

I almost laughed out loud. But then I began thinking about what that might mean—to be "very religious."

Do you think you'd have responded the same way I did? I sat wondering about what would qualify me as a religious person. The outward things? Like attending meetings, for example. If others saw me showing up for meetings, especially every Sunday, would they think of me as being very religious?

The experience of considering what it might mean to be "very religious" started me on my personal "Order of the Arrow" quest. The arrow illustration is something I use to help myself analyze what I'm doing and why and how.

How about joining me? Fill in some things on your own arrow and see what happens.

THE FLAT LINE

On the flat line, the one that stretches out horizontally across the paper, write down a bunch of things you can think of that we do as "active" (or we might say "very religious") members of The Church of Jesus Christ of Latter-day Saints.

You'll probably list some of the same things I did, such as praying, reading scriptures, attending meetings, doing our home and visiting teaching, holding family home evening, serving missions, paying tithing, fasting and paying fast offerings, doing family history work, attending the temple, memorizing the *Ensign*, singing in the ward choir, helping clean the chapel.

This might be an interesting activity for a future family home evening. Or it might not. You'll know much better than I do whether this will work for you, and in what kind of a group or setting. I'm just saying that when I've done this in company with other people, the list is much longer and the discussions are fun and stimulating.

At any rate, here you are with all these "religious activities." The DOING. There really are a bunch of them, aren't there? I've listed only a few to get you thinking and writing.

I remember someone who had recently joined the Church telling me that she'd been considered very faithful in her previous church as an "ETC Member," meaning she attended mainly on Easter, Thanksgiving, and Christmas. But once she joined the LDS Church, she said, she was busier than ever, with many more responsibilities. I felt inclined to add that there were likely many more wonderful blessings as well. But it is true that we could create a long, long list along our flat line.

THE DOWNWARD LINE

Let's now take a look at the part of the arrow that heads "south." It goes down. And the farther you travel on that line, starting at the tip and going down to the right, the more separated the line becomes from your flat line.

Let's say that this downward line is sin: doing things that we KNOW are wrong, but we do them anyway. We're off the path, committing sin—sins of commission.

It gives the illusion of being a pretty easy road: all downhill. But it isn't leading to anywhere we really want to go.

If you want, you could list some "downward-leading" things, big, little, or medium. Just include enough ideas so you remember what is indicated by this downward line. You might write things like "lie, cheat, steal, skip meetings and prayers and scripture study, ignore the Sabbath," and so on.

BACK TO THE FLAT LINE

Now I invite you to look again at the flat line. It is filled with SO many responsibilities and activities. Wow! We're so busy! Look at all we're doing!

As I looked at my flat line, I remembered that when I was a nurse, a flat line was not a good thing. It meant that someone was gone. The patient had left the room, so to speak, and wasn't coming back.

So I began to consider this line full of doing, full of actions, to be an indication *only* of being "active in the Church," whatever that might mean.

It seemed obvious that this was a far better place to be than on the downward line. But let's admit that this line may include sins of *omission.* Even with all we've written down—with all we're doing—there may be something missing, something we might call "active in the gospel."

I know this is a stretch, because there are so many wonderful things we've written down on our flat line. We're really doing many good and praiseworthy things. But maybe it's not enough just to be "very religious"—to *only* be "active in the Church." What if I've turned into "Mini Mormon" (short for Minimal Mormon), and I unconsciously (or even consciously) search for "What's the least I can do and still get into the celestial kingdom?"

Look at all I've *done!* I've read the Book of Mormon, I say my prayers every day, I know my bishop's name (and if I forget, I've got some tithing envelopes with his name printed on them to remind me), I know the first Article of Faith by heart (no prompts needed!), I wear a CTR ring, I've been on a few missions, my ancestors came across the plains, I've paid quite a bit of tithing in my life, I have a bandalo or two full of swell stuff including a daffodil, and somewhere in my house there's a copy of *Witnesses of Christ* and *The Family: A Proclamation to the World.* WOW! Hubba hubba!!

This might cause me to have a feeling of "all is well" or "I've got it made" or "Steady as she goes." There may even follow some complacency, some habitual repetition of activities and responsibilities. I may get casual about things, doing that which is most convenient and avoiding any hint of sacrifice or even deep devotion.

I may feel I'm pretty good, so what's the big deal about striving to be better? I can get "sleepy" on this flat line—pretty secure and comfortable.

It really is peculiar to try to be better when you're already pretty good. And this might be a helpful (or at least interesting and even annoying) exercise for just such a purpose. Because yes, now we come to the line that is headed up.

THE UPWARD LINE

Similar to the line that heads downward, this upward line gets farther and farther from the flat line as we project out to the right.

And, also similar to the downward line, the line heading up, up, and away is filled with things we consciously do differently. But this time we're striving to do good things, not bad things.

The line going up is headed for Heaven. This upward line has to do with the condition of my heart and soul, not just the outward activities that give me the appearance of being active in the Church, "very religious."

This direction seems to describe those who seek to deny themselves of *all* ungodliness (see Moroni 10:32) in becoming more like the Savior and our Heavenly Father. Life on this line may thus be a little more challenging than existence on either of the other two.

There is some *passion* and *animo* (the latter is a Spanish word, and I think it means good stuff in this context) in those who are on this upward line.

On the flat line, there may be a danger that we're doing

some things to receive the praise of men. We might find some competition there. Or could there be the danger of priestcraft?

The downward line brings the danger of being chained and dragged to places we do NOT want to be. We might be clever at hiding our actions (or their consequences) on this line for a while, but sooner or later we won't be able to hide anymore. This is the line and direction that leads to bondage, darkness, and misery.

There are some weaknesses in my personal version of the Order of the Arrow. For example, I might sound like I'm saying we ought to toss out everything on the flat line because it seems to be only outward stuff. But we can't do that. It's not all outward, is it? It's where we start.

I'm saying we should avoid camping on the flat line for extended periods. It could become a plateau on which we essentially stop our progress. We might get complacent. We might even get bored with our Church membership and our activities and callings.

I'm going to admit here that there may be seasons—hopefully not lasting too long—when we just have to "sit down" on the flat line for a while. Sometimes our circumstances don't seem to allow much more than that. It's critical even during these times to continue with as much as we can, praying, reading the scriptures, attending church meetings . . . whatever we can do—the best we can do.

I just point out that there is the danger of "dead works" on this flat line.

President Spencer W. Kimball warned us of this in a general

conference talk: "We have paused on some plateaus long enough. Let us resume our journey forward and upward" (*Ensign,* May 1979, 82).

When you're crossing the plains, you don't stop too long along the way.

Elder Jack H. Goaslind spoke of the same thing:

> Satan wants us to fail to reach that mountaintop that will allow us to develop a testimony so powerful that he will be unable to influence us. His work is to thwart our efforts, but the Lord has counseled us, "Fear not, little flock; do good; let earth and hell combine against you, for if ye are built upon my rock, they cannot prevail" (D&C 6:34).
>
> We have every confidence that earth and hell will not overtake you, but it will require that you move from your current plateaus and climb to higher ground.
>
> Brothers and sisters, our goodness—our every righteous endeavor—our good works, our obedience, and our efforts to bless others must be anchored in and driven by our faith in Christ, our testimonies of his mission and sacrifice, and our willingness to move off our comfortable plateaus ("Spiritual Mountaintops," *Ensign,* November 1995, 10–11).

Have you ever heard yourself say something like, "I don't know what I'd do without the gospel"? There are times when I act like I'm trying to find out. Occasionally I feel like I've lost the "zip" I've sometimes had—the passion, the level of devotion.

Another feeling that may come to us if we park or camp on this flat line is the idea that we have to "work our way to Heaven." We forget Who wants to help us.

Listen to the way Brother Stephen E. Robinson explains this: "Many of us are trying to save ourselves, holding the atonement of Jesus Christ at arm's distance and saying, 'When I've perfected myself, then I'll be worthy of the Atonement.' But that's not how it works. That's like saying, 'I won't take the medicine until I'm well. I'll be worthy of it then' " (*Ensign*, April 1992, 9).

How *sad* it is when any of us tries to go a mile or a minute alone, without seeking the help and guidance Heaven is ready, willing, and able to offer!

One of the big problems I see in being "stalled" on the flat line is that we often make comparisons that are not helpful. Think about this carefully and see if you agree with me.

From our perch in the middle, it's easy to look down and make such comments as, "Well, at least I don't . . ." In comparison with those slipping and sliding toward a dark nowhere, we seem to be pretty religious indeed.

But we also too frequently compare ourselves to those striving on the upward line. This perspective can make us very discouraged: "I can NEVER be that good!" It may also cause us to find ways to be critical of others in an effort to make ourselves feel better.

Can you see that we might compare ourselves inappropriately with those who are "perfect" OR those who are "wicked"? Do you find that happening sometimes?

I think the only measuring or comparing that is worthwhile

is personal—how am *I* doing, and am I making progress in the direction I really want to go?

We can look at different activities on the flat line to see how we're doing at getting off a plateau in some aspect of gospel living. For instance, we could look at something like fasting, which is likely skipped altogether on the downward line. On the flat line it may be that fasting means basically going without food and paying a little money. On the upward line, keeping the law of the fast could be something more meaningful and rewarding.

With scripture study, it may be that those headed downward read not at all. In my flat-line times I think I've read just to cover verses, chapters, and pages, nibbling a little bit here and there. But on the upward line there's no doubt a lot of feasting, searching, prayerful pondering, likening, and hearkening (changing).

Maybe we could examine the way we do our home or visiting teaching. Someone on the downward line might refuse to be a home or visiting teacher—or even choose not to be visited. The flat-line approach could be to "get it done," aiming for "100 percent" (whatever that means).

If we were on the upward line, maybe we would focus more on people and on watchcare, which could change the whole feeling and outcome of such important relationships.

Another example could be time. Perhaps on the downward line we KILL time. We don't show up. Time means very little if anything to us. We may take a very self-centered approach to time.

On the flat line, perhaps we WASTE time—our own and others'. It just seems to slip away.

The upward-line approach may be that we CHERISH and value time; we use it the best we can. We're grateful for it. We know it's one of God's gifts to His children.

I was imagining some possible different responses to the iron rod one day. On the downward line it felt like it might be "Rod? What Rod? Wasn't he a movie star?"

Maybe on the flat line it's something like "It's right over there," or "It's here somewhere." Or even "been there, done that."

And the upward line could be a conscious holding tightly and constantly to the iron rod.

The difference between what happens on each of the three lines might have a lot to do with our motivation. I remember a story about a queen, a crown, and a precious jewel that will help me to explain.

Once upon a time there was a beautiful queen with a magnificent queendom. She enjoyed being out with her people, and one of her favorite activities was to go to the Royal Park and play on the swings.

One evening she had been pumping hard with her plump little legs, trying to see the curve of the earth, and she made herself very tired. When she returned home to her palace and took off her crown, she realized with horror that its huge, priceless jewel had fallen out. No wonder the crown was lighter than usual! It must have been the centrifugal force created from her wild pumping!

Oh, the queen was so distraught! This priceless jewel was very important to her. She sent everyone in the castle to the park to search, but no one found the jewel.

So she sent out a proclamation to the entire queendom, notifying everyone that the jewel was missing. She offered a handsome reward to whoever could find the jewel and return it to her within thirty days. She also proclaimed that if someone found the jewel and DIDN'T return it to her within thirty days, she'd have them killed.

A few days after the loss of the jewel, a young man was in the park in the evening. There was a full moon, and he noticed something shining brightly under a bush. He got down and reached for it, and of course he discovered the queen's priceless jewel.

He sat thinking about it. He'd read the proclamation, so he knew about what the queen planned to do in the way of reward or punishment.

He finally made a decision. He took the jewel home, put it under his mattress, and waited until thirty-one days had gone by.

The next morning he took the jewel and headed for the castle. When he arrived, he asked to speak to the queen. He was informed that she was busy. He said, "It's about the jewel," whereupon he was ushered directly in to see the queen.

She was anxious for news about the jewel. He said, "I have it right here, and I've come to bring it back to you."

This pretty much took the queen's breath away. "When did you find it?" she asked.

"Just a few days after you lost it," he said.

Again, she couldn't believe his response. "Didn't you read the proclamation?" she gasped.

"Yes, I did."

Now the queen was completely puzzled. "You realize, then, that had you returned the jewel yesterday I would have rewarded you handsomely."

"Yes, I realize that."

"Then you must also realize that since you waited until today, I can have you killed."

"Yes, I read that on the proclamation too."

Shaking her head in disbelief, the queen asked, "Then WHY did you wait until today?"

The young man explained that when he found the jewel, he wondered about his motivation for returning it right away. He didn't want to be motivated by the hope for a reward. But he also didn't want to be motivated to return the jewel because he was afraid not to.

"I'm returning this jewel to you today," said the young man, "not because I'm hoping for a reward, and not because I'm afraid not to, but because it's the right thing to do. It belongs to you."

And that's the story. I think the young man lived a long and happy life, but that's not part of what I wanted to share. I want the story to help us look at our motivation for what we choose to do with our life, our time.

On the downward line, I think there is probably a frequent sense of fear, even if it is kept hidden as much as possible. We'd likely find some darkness, noise, hopelessness, dead ends, and so on. There perhaps is even an effort to pull others down. What is it they say? Misery loves company!

Also on this downward line there may be a feeling of, "I couldn't care less; let's party!" There may be a focus on physical pleasures, with no restraint, boundaries, or self-discipline. Nothing is sacred, and nothing is wrong. There are the habits of the natural man (an enemy to God) working for the plan of MISERY. Consequences may seem out of the picture, but they're on their way. All of the pleasures of the downward line will melt eventually into misery.

On the flat line we might find the hope of a great reward for all the activity, and also a great sense of duty—tracking the numbers and being busy and perhaps competing quite a bit. There may also be a lot of GUILT on this line. Again—if we're focusing only on what we're DOING, we may be experiencing sins of omission.

And likely on the upward line there is a sense of doing what is right because it's right and good. Those moving upward no longer have to be commanded in all things. They are happily engaged in doing good and being good. The motivation is from within, not without. The upward line is where we become instruments in the hands of God, seeking to know what He wants us to do. When we ask, "What would Jesus do?" we really mean it, and we do our best to respond to the answer. We aren't perfect yet, but we're progressing in that direction.

I think we might say that the flat line is a line of "should," "have to," and even "need to," while the upward line is "want to" and "love to."

The upward line is filled with a sense of faith, hope, charity, peace, serenity, happiness! It's doing many of the very things that are on the flat line, but with a different depth of feeling and meaning. There seems to have come a moment when all the flat-line doing began to have an incredible meaning and purpose, bringing more joy than we thought possible.

On the flat line we may be calling attention to ourselves: "Look at all I'm doing! Look at all I've done!" On the upward line it's more like being aware of "who I'm becoming, without any arrogance." Could it be that our efforts on the upward line are an indication of what we really hold most precious and dear in our lives?

Although there doesn't seem to be the same need for credit or praise or notice for goodness or service or obedience on the upward line, it's hard to hide what's happening to us. A countenance "betrays" a person for his or her goodness as well as for the opposite.

Read the words of Isaiah from 2 Nephi 13:9, and think of what might happen to our countenance if we remain on the downward path: "The show of their countenance doth witness against them, and doth declare their sin to be even as Sodom, and they cannot hide it. Wo unto their souls, for they have rewarded evil unto themselves!"

Part of our countenance, the light that comes from within, from what and who we really are, is our smiles. I ran across an interesting quote about smiles from eighteenth-century Swiss theologian Johann Kaspar Lavater: "There are many kinds of smiles, each having a distinct character. Some announce goodness and sweetness, others betray sarcasm, bitterness, and pride; some soften the countenance by their languishing tenderness, others brighten by their spiritual vivacity."

He also said: "There are three classes of men: the retrograde, the stationary and the progressive." That's an interesting thought in light of our three lines, isn't it?

Elder Robert L. Simpson wrote:

> We do right for various reasons. Some people do right simply because they don't want to be punished for doing wrong. When we do right for fear of retribution, I think our foundation is very shaky.
>
> Another might say, "I want to do right because I have always been taught that this is the thing to do." Well, such reasoning is based on hearsay, on the testimony of others, and I think we need to mature beyond that point. I think we need to have our own testimonies instead of the advice of others on a perpetual basis.
>
> Others have been heard to say, "I want to do right just to please my parents," and although we all should have a desire to please our parents, that reason alone is not sufficient to sustain us throughout eternity.
>
> Perhaps you have heard people who have indicated that they are doing the right thing simply because they want to be obedient to God's commands; this, too, is a very high and noble purpose—provided,

> of course, that that obedience is not blind obedience, without personal conviction.
>
> But to me the best reason of all is illustrated by the person who feels the desire to do right because he wants to add glory to his Father in heaven.
>
> Whatever stage of motivation we find ourselves in, I think we must eventually reinforce this with our own personal testimony that has been built on a foundation of gospel scholarship and understanding—a testimony which leads us to the life of unselfishness and service, one which finds its highest sanctification in the supreme thought that we are living gospel principles because we desire to glorify his great name ("Cast Your Burden upon the Lord," *New Era,* January 1977, 4).

I like the way Elder Simpson invites us to examine our stage of motivation (maybe as the young man who found the queen's priceless jewel did) and to reinforce it with our own personal testimony.

How do we move from one line to another? Not easily, I suspect, even if we're going, say, from the flat line to the downward line. I think it would not be easy to give up so much. I think misery would be increased and darkness deepened if we had known better, had tasted the sweet. It seems like the things that pull us to the downward line include pride, greed, selfishness, and doubt.

If we're wanting to move up from the downward line to the flat line, it's a matter of repenting. Changing.

And going from the flat line to the upper line probably

requires a change of heart, some consecration, sacrifice, and genuine goodness. We get to the upper line when we come unto Christ—when we follow Him, and when we allow Him to show us our weaknesses, then accept His help in overcoming them.

We saw earlier that the distance between the flat line and the upward line increases the farther we travel on the upward line. Let's talk about another kind of difference in some lines.

Years ago there was a great commotion in the land about the use of a swear word in the movie *Gone with the Wind.* I'm going to pretend that most of the people in the USA were pretty shocked by that, and I invite you to imagine a line representing the level on which most people were living. There were fairly common standards of conduct and decency at that level.

It may be that at the time, Latter-day Saints held even higher standards than that. Just for the sake of this little discussion, let's say that the line representing Church members was two inches higher than the "normal" line. A difference of two inches doesn't mean much, but I just want to show us going along a couple of inches higher than most people, with some stricter standards and some things we held sacred that perhaps weren't as sacred to others.

Then began a great decline that is sliding downward faster and faster—not just in movies, but in television, magazines, online stuff, books, conversations, plays, and other things we could mention. The shock over that line from *Gone with the Wind* is pretty much gone with the passing of time.

So where are WE? If we're striving to be better—as a church, not just individually—we shouldn't still be only two inches above that down-sliding line. Should we?

If we're improving—if we're becoming more obedient, more faithful, shouldn't we be headed upward? What kind of celebration could we have for still being only two inches above everyone else at this point in time?

Let me take another crack at explaining this concept by talking about the cost of gasoline. I remember getting a gallon of gas for nineteen cents, and some readers will remember an even lower price. As years have passed, the price has been going up, until now it's a source of real concern in a person's and family's budget.

One day I was filling my car and noticed that the price, which had been close to $3.00 a gallon, had been going lower. On this particular day it was something like $2.849 per gallon. I caught myself thinking, "Wow—it's only $2.849 a gallon!"

My point is, I realized I was getting excited about a price that would have horrified me just a few years earlier. Even in January 2002 I could get gas for just over $1.00 a gallon.

I'm just saying that we should be ascending, not slipping into habits that seem "tame" compared to what others are doing, but are actually awful when compared to what and HOW we want to be. We should be neither excited nor content that we're "two inches higher" or "only $2.849 a gallon." What that really means is that we've been slipping along with everyone else. We're letting go of things too—things we should have been holding onto tightly (like an iron rod, for example).

As Elder Neal A. Maxwell said, "In so many respects, the

world's ways head in opposite directions from gospel destinations" ("Popularity and Principle," *Ensign,* March 1995, 12). The gaps make us sad rather than proud. We don't like moving away from others, especially loved ones.

As difficult as it may be, is there a step you are willing to take to go from a flat line to an upward line? IS IT TIME? Can we keep doing the same thing over and over in the same way and really expect different results? Without a change in what we're *doing,* there can be no change in who we're *becoming.*

Let's talk about this online (see page 198). Look through some of the many things you've written down, and let's share with each other. I look forward to finding out what you're thinking and feeling about all of this.

I realize that much of this is simplistic, but I hope it will provide a chance to do some pondering about direction, priorities, motivation, and all. The invitation "COME UNTO ME" is an invitation to "COME ON UP!" This is the direction that leads ultimately to consecration and "Thy will be done."

HIGHLY RECOMMENDED READING

Boy Scout Handbook (just kidding . . . except that I've read a lot about Scouting, and I've come away with some great ideas!)

Charles Sheldon, *In His Steps,* Uhrichsville, OH: Barbour Publishing, Inc., 2002.

Neal A. Maxwell, "Popularity and Principle," *Ensign,* March 1995, 12–15.

CHAPTER 4

Striving to Be Better When You're Already Pretty Good

Have you ever wished you were a car? Wouldn't it be great if you could pull into some station every two or three thousand miles to get your oil changed and your tires rotated? They'd check all the fluid levels, test your brakes, make sure you had enough tread on your tires for the roads ahead, and be certain that the battery was strong enough to make it through a long winter. Maybe there would be a coupon so that it wouldn't cost an arm and a leg to get spiffed up.

Sometimes I wish I were a car. If I were, I'd like to be something nice and fancy—probably a 1952 Hudson. Mrs. Swan, who used to sell Guardian Service pans to my mother, drove a Hudson of about that vintage. I think I'm looking more and more like a Hudson than a Ferrari, if you know what I mean.

But we're not cars. Sing it: "You're not a car."

As I wander around different neighborhoods and talk to lots of people, I have the feeling that many of us would need an oil change if we WERE cars. Fan belts are thin, fluid levels are low, tread is almost gone on the tires, and the battery has needed a few charges in recent months. Thank goodness for the cables we keep in our trunk!

And OH, the trunk! There should be a charge (speaking of charges) just for getting to look inside each others' trunks. Wow. The stuff we've collected!

I'm saying that many of us are what I would call "stressed out." Overwhelmed. Trying to carry very heavy burdens.

I've given MUCH thought to all of this, wondering how we can make needed changes in order to experience more JOY, more PEACE, more mornings when we actually feel like getting up, more evenings when we feel like we've made a positive difference in the world that day.

I don't think we enjoy ourselves enough. Has it been a while since you really enjoyed yourself? Enjoyed YOU?

Do you like yourself? Are you happy with who you are and where you are?

I wish more people could and would answer "yes" (even if not enthusiastically for right now) when I ask questions like those. But the truth is, I think there are many of us who almost constantly wish we were someone else. We even go to great effort and expense—of time and emotion as much as of money—to become someone else.

Maybe that's why a lot of people get caught up in other people's lives, even the lives of fictitious people on TV, in movies, in magazines and books. "OH! If only I could have a life like that!" they think.

But guess what, friends? Our striving to be better is what brings the very happiness and peace we are searching for! Happiness doesn't happen because of money or a huge home or being on the cover of a magazine or having photographers and reporters following us around. It comes from inside of us—from our hearts and the desires that are most precious to us. It comes from GOODNESS. That's what lessens our stress and anxiety, our feeling of being overwhelmed. That's what keeps us aware of the direction we're going and of the Heavenly help that is so near—the "straight-and-narrow refreshment stands" along the way.

Think back to that arrow—lines going up and down, and that flat one in the middle. Once you get these three lines in your mind, you can do some soul-searching. You can take a topic and discover some ways to "step up"—ways to try a little harder to be a little better.

I'll never forget the feeling I had when President Gordon B. Hinckley first shared that phrase. He made so many impossible dreams possible! I remember thinking more like the little engine that could—trying a little harder to be a little better was the kind of invitation I needed.

I want to put that invitation from President Hinckley in a broader context from one of the times he used it. It was April conference, 1995, and he had been the prophet for just a few days. He said:

> Now, my beloved brethren and sisters, as we return to our homes, may we go . . . with determination to

> try a little harder to be a little better. Please know that we are not without understanding of some of your problems. We are aware that many of you carry very heavy burdens. We plead with the Lord in your behalf. We add our prayers to your prayers that you may find solutions to your problems. We leave a blessing upon you, even an apostolic blessing. We bless you that the Lord may smile with favor upon you, that there may be happiness and peace in your homes and in your lives, that an atmosphere of love and respect and appreciation may be felt among husbands and wives, children and parents. May you "look to God and live" (Alma 37:47) with happiness, with security, with peace, with faith ("We Have a Work to Do," *Ensign,* May 1995, 88).

Part of what I love about this quote is knowing that our leaders, including our prophet, plead with the Lord for us. President Hinckley left an apostolic blessing on that beautiful day in April and asked that the Lord would smile upon us. He understands more about our challenges and problems than we likely realize.

Even so, he asks us to be better. As we strive to get off any plateaus on which we may have paused, we are following a prophet's invitation. We really are trying to be a little better.

Some people have trouble with the word *try.* Some feel it's a word that allows us to not work quite as hard. But I actually like the word. Listen to the way President Howard W. Hunter gave counsel using *try:*

> We should at every opportunity ask ourselves, "What would Jesus do?" and then be more courageous to act upon the answer. We must follow Christ, in the best sense of that word. We must be about his work as he was about his Father's. We should try to be like him, even as the Primary children sing, "Try, try, try" (*Children's Songbook,* p. 55). To the extent that our mortal powers permit, we should make every effort to become like Christ—the one perfect and sinless example this world has ever seen ("What Manner of Men Ought Ye to Be?" *Ensign,* May 1994, 64).

One important aspect of trying to be like Jesus is the realization that this is the direction of the upward line—we're seeking to become more like the Savior and our Heavenly Father, denying ourselves increasingly of all that is ungodly, because we know it's the only way to reach the most wonderful of destinations—to return Home. With that in mind, let's look more closely at some of the things on the flat line that we might move to the upward line by trying a little harder.

PRAYER

One of the flat-line activities I've been working on in my own life is the quality of my personal prayers. I'd love to know what your thoughts are as to the types of prayer on each line.

On the downward line it may be that prayer is what people turn to only when they need help, if then. "I'm in a foxhole! Help!"

On the flat line, where I find myself too often, I "say my

prayers." Much of the time I do so out of habit or routine. Do you ever find yourself realizing that your prayers have lost something? Sometimes when I hear someone else pray, or read an article or talk about prayer, I realize that I've slipped—that my personal prayers are not nearly deep enough or earnest enough. At times they're even boring!

I know the difference. I know it well. I've had some extremely sweet and meaningful conversations with my Heavenly Father. I've received important counsel as I've been willing to take time, to be real, to listen.

President James E. Faust taught: "A fervent, sincere prayer is a two-way communication that will do much to bring the Spirit flowing like healing water to help with the trials, hardships, aches, and pains we all face. What is the quality of our secret prayers? As we pray, we should think of our Heavenly Father as being close by; full of knowledge, understanding, love, and compassion; the essence of power; and having great expectations of each of us" ("That We Might Know Thee," *Ensign*, January 1999, 2, 4).

Our Father in Heaven *does* have great expectations of us—He wants us to come back Home to be with Him forever! And He is ready, willing, and able to help with that process.

Once when I had accidentally watched the news, I had become quite sad about all the trouble in the world. I was likely feeling rather helpless, and I was talking to myself out loud about the whole thing. At some point I said in despair, "All I can do is pray."

Almost instantly it was as if the Spirit whispered to me, "I beg your pardon?" Oooops. I tried to ignore the question. But another whispering came: "What did you just say?"

"Well, I said that all I could was pray about all the terrible things that are happening in the world."

"As if prayer isn't effective—as if it doesn't make any difference?"

"No, I guess I didn't really mean that. . . ."

"You think there are other things that help more?"

"Maybe I was feeling that."

"Are you having other thoughts now?"

"Yes."

"Want to share?"

"Well, I'm realizing that when I pray with real intent, with all my heart, and I really mean what I'm saying—what I'm asking—I'm pleading with Heavenly Father to send help. And I know He does. I really do know that."

"Whew. Good. It was nice visiting with you."

MEETINGS

We could look at attendance at meetings and see what the difference might be on the three lines. We have a lot of meetings, don't we? It likely seems peculiar to others that we voluntarily go to so many meetings.

I love what some have called the "14th Article of Faith": "We believe in meetings—all that have been scheduled, all that are now scheduled, and we believe that there will yet be many great and important meetings scheduled. We have endured many meetings and hope to be able to endure all meetings.

Indeed we may say that if there is a meeting, or anything that resembles a meeting, or anything that we might possibly turn into a meeting, we seek after these things."

On the downward line, maybe people seldom if ever attend meetings. Maybe some have been away so long that it feels too awkward even to think of returning.

On the flat line, I may attend, but perhaps I've not invested anything except my time. My body is there, propped on the bench, but my spirit is wandering.

I remember coming out of a sacrament meeting years ago and hearing my sister Charlotte say what a great meeting it had been. I thought she'd taken ill! Looking back, I think she was on a different line than I was. I was a flat-line meeting attender. I was finished with the meeting long before the last "amen."

On the upward line I may be listening attentively, learning, resolving to make some changes, taking notes (which helps me listen better), lending my spirit and encouragement to those who are speaking or participating in other ways, and so on.

Part of attendance at sacrament meeting would be the spirit and feeling with which I partake of the sacrament. It may be that if I'm on a flat-line course I would just do it automatically, not thinking about anything in particular. I would think those on the upward part of the arrow would strive to have a meaningful experience in renewing baptismal covenants and drawing closer to the Savior.

Upward-line meeting attendance also might include letting someone know that they helped you in some way—that they gave you something to think about, or reminded you of an important principle, or helped you worship more effectively.

I had an experience that illustrates some of these ideas. One Sunday in January 2002, I noticed my neighbor Ben Hanks near the door of the chapel after our meetings had finished. I had been meaning to talk to him, and I asked if he had a minute. "Sure," he said.

I told him about the first Sunday in December, a few weeks before that. I had wanted to have a meaningful experience partaking of the sacrament. I'd been thinking about it, praying about it, reading some scriptures and hymns, and hoping for a good experience.

I went to sacrament meeting early, and once again began reading the words of hymns and some scriptures, doing what I could to help put myself in a position to have a very positive experience in partaking of the sacrament and renewing sacred covenants.

I told Ben that I had sung the sacrament hymn thinking carefully about the words, and then had closed my eyes and waited to listen intently to the words of the prayer. The priest began.

I said: "For some reason it seemed to me that the priest who was offering the prayer was going more slowly or more carefully, or both. He seemed to be thinking about what he was saying, and it didn't sound like he was reading. It helped me so much!"

I admitted that I had opened my eyes immediately following "amen" to see who had been the one to offer that prayer so beautifully. "It was YOU, Ben," I told him, and then I thanked him sincerely for helping me to have what I had wanted—a meaningful experience partaking of the sacrament that day.

Ben, who had just turned sixteen a few weeks earlier, had been watching and listening intently. When I finished, he said: "It was my first time, and I'd been thinking a lot about it. I wanted to do it right. I didn't want to just read what was on the card—I wanted it to be meaningful. I wanted to think about what I was saying." And then he added, "I wondered if anyone would notice."

Oh my goodness. What if I hadn't noticed? Or what if I had noticed, but I hadn't said anything?

Heavenly Father noticed, and He helped me notice, and He also prompted me to say something about it to Ben.

This is part of what is meant by lending our spirits and our encouragement to others. We may make more of a difference than we can even imagine.

Speaking again about meetings and other opportunities, I've heard some say that general conference is just the "same old thing" twice a year. Ouch. Or even the temple: "Same old, same old."

What can we do if we're the ones feeling that way? Elder Boyd K. Packer gave some counsel that might help: "I say again, FOLLOW THE BRETHREN. In a few days there opens another general conference of the Church. The servants of the Lord will counsel us. You may listen with anxious ears and hearts, or you may turn that counsel aside. As [with other meetings], what you shall gain will depend not so much upon their preparation of the messages as upon your preparation for them" ("Follow the Brethren," *Tambuli*, September 1979, 63).

Isn't his counsel powerful? It gives me a lot to think about to have him tell me that my preparation for the messages makes such a difference!

CALLED TO SERVE

It's interesting to observe how different people accept callings to serve. Any and all opportunities to serve provide the chance to respond from the upward line.

I think of Elaine L. Jack, who, when she was released as Relief Society general president, became Primary pianist in her ward. And she loved it!

Think of people you know who have been bishops and are now working in the nursery, teaching Scouts, or serving in some other important way.

It's true, as has been said in different ways, that what matters is not where we serve but how. President Thomas S. Monson often shares this poem by Meade McGuire that expresses this sentiment so well:

> "Father, where shall I work today?"
> And my love flowed warm and free.
> Then He pointed out a tiny spot
> And said, "Tend that for me."
> I answered quickly, "Oh no; not that!
> Why, no one would ever see,
> No matter how well my work was done;
> Not that little place for me."
> And the word He spoke, it was not stern;
> He answered me tenderly:

"Ah, little one, search that heart of thine.
Art thou working for them or for me?
Nazareth was a little place,
And so was Galilee."
(In "The Call of Duty," *Ensign,* May 1986, 39)

One thing we can't afford to indulge in is the "been there, done that" kind of attitude. Maybe you've noticed this happening. Someone will say, "I've already worked in Primary," or, "I've already been a Scout leader; my hiking and camping days are behind me now." There can be many variations, such as "I've already done girls' camp," "I've been in three elders quorum presidencies already," or "I've already taught in Relief Society enough—let the young ones have a turn." That's right—many actually express the thought that "It's someone else's turn now."

President Hinckley never said, "I've already dedicated a temple. Let someone else go to Chile and Newport Beach." He never murmured about having spoken in general conference more than 200 times, or whined about having to travel another 20,000 miles to visit members in places where he could have said, "I've already been there. I don't want to go back to Africa" (or Asia, or South America, or anywhere else). And he certainly didn't use his ninety-fifth birthday party to announce he was retiring as prophet—that it had become just too much responsibility for someone his age.

What can you say about someone who has given his whole life to serving God and His children? "We ever pray for thee, our prophet dear" (*Hymns,* no. 23).

Interestingly, when we receive and accept callings, we are *set apart*. Do you remember that phrase as being one definition of *peculiar*? What if part of the significance of that "setting apart" is that we are separated from what (or who) we were before the calling came to us?

ENDURING TO THE END

Enduring to the end is part of the deal here on earth. Eternal life comes to those who endure to the end. Just one of many examples of that promise appears in 2 Nephi 31:20: "Wherefore, ye must press forward with a steadfastness in Christ, having a perfect brightness of hope, and a love of God and of all men. Wherefore, if ye shall press forward, feasting upon the word of Christ, and endure to the end, behold, thus saith the Father: Ye shall have eternal life."

On the downward line, there may not be much ability to endure even for an hour or a day.

On the flat line the enduring process may include a touch of Martyr Complex. Enduring is a duty, a chore, practically devoid of joy and peace.

Those I've observed enduring who are on the upward line have a sense of peace that is contagious. In spite of challenges, they seem cheerful, positive, and grateful. I've sometimes thought that was so weird! Maybe those upward-line folks possess an ability to look ahead and press forward with confidence in the Savior and a perfect brightness of hope.

The 23rd Psalm expresses much of what I feel about the help we receive through the hours, days, weeks, months, and years of our lives. Someday when you have a chance, read that beautiful psalm again.

Many of our hymns are also very encouraging. Try reading the words to some of these:

"Be Still, My Soul," no. 124

"Does the Journey Seem Long?" no. 127

"Cast Thy Burden upon the Lord," no. 110

"Come unto Jesus," no. 117

"Come, Ye Disconsolate," no. 115

I could go on and on. Let the words of the hymns be a source of help and comfort as you endure your trials and carry your burdens.

Never forget that your Heavenly Father and the Savior know how you are feeling in all the burdens that are so heavy for you right now. They understand your loneliness, your joy, your tears, your heartaches, and your striving.

THE WORD OF WISDOM

Another thing we might try a little harder at is keeping the Word of Wisdom. Here is one commandment that can cause us to stand out and really be peculiar. You have likely been in circumstances where you were the only one not participating in "happy hour" or trying drugs or starting the morning with a cup of coffee.

Those on the downward line may have some problems in this area, but they're not the only ones, are they?

On my flat line, ask me if I "keep" the Word of Wisdom, and

I'll say, "of course!"—meaning that I don't drink coffee or smoke.

But here's something peculiar: There is much more to the Word of Wisdom than some "don'ts," isn't there? What would it take for you to be on the upward line in regards to the Word of Wisdom? There are some very positive "do it" things.

And oh, the promises! Including the ability to run and not be weary and walk and not faint. And isn't it wonderful to know that God is pleased both with those who run and with those who walk? He just wants us to do all we can—the best we can do.

Here are some other concepts that might be interesting and meaningful to consider on your own or as you study and ponder with others:

AGENCY

PERSONAL WORSHIP

TEMPLE ATTENDANCE

Elder David B. Haight had something to say about our striving to be better when we're already pretty good:

> The time is now to rededicate our lives to eternal ideals and values, to make those changes that we may need to make in our own lives and conduct to conform to the Savior's teachings.
>
> From the beginning to the end of His ministry, Jesus asked His followers to adopt new, higher standards in contrast to their former ways. As believers, they were to live by a spiritual and moral code that would separate them not only from the rest of the

> world but also even from some of their traditions. He asks nothing less of those who follow Him today ("Ethics and Honesty," *Ensign*, November 1987, 15).

And as President Gordon B. Hinckley has taught, "You have bypassed the things of the world. You are on your way to something higher and better. . . . You are something special. You must rise above the ordinary" ("Some Thoughts on Temples, Retention of Converts, and Missionary Service," *Ensign*, November 1997, 52).

I'm convinced that the more we strive to become who we really are—children of God with the potential to become as He is—the more we will seem unique to those who may be choosing a different direction.

HIGHLY RECOMMENDED READING

Joseph B. Wirthlin, "Seeking the Good," *Ensign*, May 1992, 86–88.

Virginia H. Pearce, *A Heart Like His*, Salt Lake City: Deseret Book, 2006.

CHAPTER 5

Vital Signs

Is it just MEE, or is time going faster now than it used to? Are the years flying by for you too? Lately it seems like there are only a few days between the Fourth of July and Halloween. Whooosh! And Christmas decorations are sneaked into the stores a little earlier every year. I figure they save on storage costs and space by just putting everything behind some doors or under a blanket for a few weeks.

Turning calendar pages or tearing them off has become almost a part-time job—something I feel I do way too often.

One of the ways I measure the passing of time is to be aware of anniversaries—birthdays, holidays, and other significant events. Once I had a hilarious calendar that made up holidays for every single day of the year—things like hair-braiding demonstrations, anthill beautifying contests, and the annual rabbit round-up festival somewhere between Ely and Elko.

I wish I could find that calendar again. Maybe it's in the basement with my Ferdinand Marcos martial-law poster, my copy of *Jude the Obscure*, my nightgown from when I was in Taiwan, and the Vietnam boots (they had actually been worn in the war) that I bought at a Relief Society bazaar in the Philippines.

(Sidetrack: I have to tell you of an incident in bringing the Vietnam boots home back in 1973. When I got to the airport, I was carrying them. The people at the airline said I couldn't do that, so I said I'd put them on if that would be better. They did fit over my shoes. When the airline folks realized I was serious—I had stooped down to start the process—they let me carry them.)

On my own I remember things like 06 April as a day of many anniversaries, including the birth of the Savior, and 28 December as the day my dad went Home. And 08 June 1978 is a day I'll never forget, with the joyful news that all worthy male members of the Church could receive the priesthood and participate in all ordinances.

For some reason I always remember things like Pearl Harbor Day on 07 December and the terrible tragedy on 9/11 in 2001. I remember that the day after Christmas in 2004 the tsunami struck.

I remember how long it's been since I served as a missionary—the dates of beginning and finishing are marked deeply, even though with each passing year they are further and further away.

Time does go by, doesn't it? Happy days eventually become "remember when" stories, just as the not-so-happy days do.

My favorite time of year begins sometime in September when that autumn feeling is in the air and the leaves begin their magic color changes. Things like bears and garden spots prepare to hibernate for the winter.

I absolutely love the anticipation of Christmas and the other holidays, followed by another brand-new year.

The end of the year and the beginning of a new one is quite an event for me. I used to celebrate with my friends, staying up all night to eat, play games, bang on pans at midnight, and light a firecracker if I could talk my brother Paul into giving me one from his stash. I think he had a connection in Wyoming, because he always had a fantastic supply.

These days I sleep through the midnight hour. (What a wimp!) Somehow it still seems to me, though, like it should take longer than a moment at the stroke of midnight to say good-bye and hello.

This new beginning each 365 days or so reminds me of something I used to do a LOT as a nurse: take "vital signs." They gave an indication of how the patient was doing. These vital signs included what we called "TPR": temperature, pulse, and rate of respirations.

If there were patients who were lacking any of these vital signs, or if the numbers were too high or too low, there was trouble. For example, if there were no pulse . . . you get the idea. Vital signs are called that because they really are VITAL.

It was important for me as a nurse to know what the vital signs SHOULD be, or I would have had no idea whether the patient was doing all right or needed some help.

In a way, the end of one year and the beginning of a new one is a good opportunity for us to check our own "vital signs." It's a time of reflection, certainly—not just "How did this year go by so quickly!" but "How well did I use it? How close did I come to reaching some of the goals I set?"

There's something about the passing of time that brings such questions to my mind. "How have I changed since __________?" And then I'll think of some experience, some event, some moment or season in my life. Sometimes the question is about feelings and details I may have let go of as time has gone by. I find I've forgotten things that I was pretty positive I would never forget.

Many people like to set goals and make resolutions at the beginning of each year. I think that's a good idea. And I guess looking at my vital signs turns out to be about the same thing.

Some people and families do this in a pretty formal way, writing things down and checking them off, and even making charts and graphs with flashing lights, bells, whistles, and rewards hidden under stickers.

I'm not quite that formal, although I do keep track of a few things. And yes, in anticipation of your question, I do a better job of keeping track in the first weeks of a new year than I do as the months go by.

One good question is: What ARE my vital signs? What do I consider not just important or wonderful or good in my life, but vital—essential? It's an interesting exercise for me to list as many of these things as I can think of and then see if I use my year focusing enough on them (or focusing at all on them). The very acts of making lists, setting goals, and doing something different often help dispel discouragement and even boredom.

My own vital signs include prayer, scriptures, temple attendance, time and influence with my family, being grateful, keeping covenants and other promises, keeping the Sabbath day holy, and seeking the constant influence of the Holy Ghost. I set many other goals, of course, but those are some of the VITAL things. I guess the other goals are important because they have such an impact on the vital things.

So as not to be overwhelmed, maybe we could make a plan for the coming year in which we focus on strengthening one area that is vital to our wholeness. It may be that we add another prayer to our day, maybe a thank-you prayer in the middle of the day.

We might decide to go to the temple more often than we were able to go last year, and think of specific ways in which we can be better prepared to enjoy the experience and be responsive to spiritual impressions.

Another vital thing might be to seek for more meaningful experiences each week as we partake of the sacrament and renew our baptismal covenants. I've tried doing this, mostly in "spurts," and I know that having this as a goal for an entire year would make a noticeable difference in my life.

I find it helps if I do more than just write down "prayer," or "scriptures," or "temple." It helps me personally to consider some specific strategies for making such vital things more meaningful, more enjoyable, and more purposeful.

For example, if I'm working to develop a deeper, stronger faith, it isn't particularly helpful to set a goal like "get more faith." My goal is more meaningful if I work to cultivate a closeness to the Savior, specifically to develop more faith and trust in Him. Aspects of my goal can be to study more about how to do this, and to read and listen to examples of how others have done it or are doing it. I like to ask people I respect how they've worked on some of their personal goals.

I used the word *cultivate* in that last paragraph, and it's a word I've been noticing more often in the past four or nine years or so. I've been noticing how often President Gordon B. Hinckley uses that very word, *cultivate.* That in itself makes it a wonderful analogy, knowing something of President Hinckley's love for working in the yard and garden, cultivating the ground, planting, irrigating, weeding, watching things grow, and harvesting.

I've noticed that the word is often used in connection with words such as develop, strengthen, consciously pursue, focus on.

The word *cultivate* means "to till." It's like preparing for crops—to manure, plow, dress, sow, and reap. It also means: "To improve by labor or study; to advance the growth of; to refine and improve by correction of faults, and enlargement of powers or good qualities; as, to *cultivate* talents; to *cultivate* a taste for poetry."

We can also *cultivate* the mind.

"To *cultivate* is to cherish; to foster; to labor to promote and increase; as, to *cultivate* the love of excellence; to *cultivate* gracious affections; to improve" (*An American Dictionary of the English Language,* Noah Webster, 1828, electronic edition, © 1998 Deseret Book Company).

So when we're working to cultivate a quality, a characteristic, or a pattern of living, it means we pay attention to it, acquire it, cherish it, improve it, and develop it. We focus on promoting our growth in areas we choose. We can cultivate our imagination, our patience, our sense of humor, our manners, our honesty and integrity, or anything else that is of value to us.

Cultivating is part of the law of the harvest. That which we plant is what grows and what we are able to harvest. As Sister Elaine Cannon taught, "Another thing that we can count on is that neither here nor hereafter are we suddenly going to emerge with qualities we haven't developed or a pattern of living for which we have not prepared ourselves" ("Reach for Joy," *Ensign,* May 1982, 95).

To cultivate includes sinking our roots deep into the doctrines and principles that are part of the gospel of Jesus Christ. The Apostle Paul taught that persistence is necessary in serving, as it is in planting and harvesting. "And let us not be weary in well doing: for in due season we shall reap, if we faint not. As we have therefore opportunity, let us do good unto all" (Galatians 6:9–10).

I ran across an interesting article by Elder William H. Bennett in an *Ensign*. The title was what caught my attention: “Inertia.” In it, he shared this quotation from Richard L. Evans:

> Some *things* we inherit. Some *things* are passed to us from others. But this doesn’t make of *us* anything we aren’t. We may enjoy the talents of others, but this doesn’t develop our own. We do not suddenly become what we do not cooperate in becoming. We do not learn well what we are not willing to learn.
>
> In indifference, some things may remain in our minds, some things may attach themselves to us. But generally what we are, what we do, what we become is because we were willing to put in for what we want to get out.
>
> Basically we always were. And what we shall be is what we are, plus what we add to it—always and forever. And there would be no better time than now to decide to learn, to do, to develop, to work, to improve, to produce, to increase our competence, to extend ourselves in service (“Inertia,” *Ensign*, May 1974, 34).

I’d like to share some of the quotations I like best about cultivating different attributes, and then give a few ideas on how we might go about working on them. I have listed them in no particular order of importance, but I chose them because they seem relevant to our goal of cultivating vital Godlike and Christlike attributes.

BE OF GOOD CHEER

Of course I want to begin this little section with a couple of scriptures. The first is one of my 1000 favorites.

"Wherefore, be of good cheer, and do not fear, for I the Lord am with you, and will stand by you; and ye shall bear record of me, even Jesus Christ, that I am the Son of the living God, that I was, that I am, and that I am to come" (Doctrine and Covenants 68:6).

I remember Elder Jacob deJager speaking to a group of us who were serving as missionaries in Indonesia, and in his wonderfully expressive way he told us that "be of good cheer" was not a suggestion, it was a commandment!

President Gordon B. Hinckley has shared so much about being of good cheer. At the general women's meeting on 29 September 1984, he quoted the Lord's words, "Wherefore, lift up thy heart and rejoice, and cleave unto the covenants which thou hast made" (D&C 25:13). He then said:

> I believe he is saying to each of us, be happy. The gospel is a thing of joy. It provides us with a reason for gladness. Of course there are times of sorrow. Of course there are hours of concern and anxiety. We all worry. But the Lord has told us to lift our hearts and rejoice. I see so many people, including many women, who seem never to see the sunshine, but who constantly walk with storms under cloudy skies. Cultivate an attitude of happiness. Cultivate a spirit of optimism. Walk with faith, rejoicing in the

> beauties of nature, in the goodness of those you love, in the testimony which you carry in your heart concerning things divine ("If Thou Art Faithful," *Ensign*, November 1984, 91–92).

What a fantastic invitation from a prophet! "Cultivate an attitude of happiness. Cultivate a spirit of optimism." He asks that we cultivate a spirit of gladness in our homes, and that we let the light of the gospel shine in our faces wherever we go and in whatever we do.

These are some fruits—some consequences—of living the gospel of Jesus Christ the best we can. We experience good cheer, optimism, gladness, happiness, and pure joy!

Elder Jack H. Goaslind has taught: "Words such as *reap*, *restored*, and *desire* imply that happiness is a consequence, not a reward. We are *restored* to a state of happiness when we have chosen to live according to the plan of happiness. Our joy in God's kingdom will be a natural extension of the happiness we cultivate in this life. . . . Striving for happiness is a long, hard journey with many challenges. It requires eternal vigilance to win the victory. You cannot succeed with sporadic little flashes of effort" ("Happiness," *Ensign*, May 1986, 53).

So here is our challenge—we are invited and encouraged to cultivate good cheer, happiness, optimism, and good humor. But how? What if I was born moody? What if I'm almost always depressed? What if my parents were negative and pessimistic? What if my friends are mostly "down"? What if I hate my job? What if I'm trapped with laundry, wiggly little children, never enough time, and a grumpy husband at the end of each day?

One thing I've found in my personal quest for good cheer is that I am entirely too quick to blame others for my lack of joy and optimism. The absence of gladness in my life is because of the weather, or a rude person on the bus, or the fact that they still haven't fixed the faucet in the women's rest room, or the reality of another bad hair day.

Do you see what I mean? I'm acting as if—and living as if—happiness comes from the outside. I can't begin to cultivate it effectively until I recognize and admit that it comes from the inside. It's up to me!

I love the *Peanuts* cartoon I saw years ago where a frowning Lucy is declaring that whoever is in charge of her happiness isn't doing a good job. In truth, SHE is the one who isn't doing a good job, because she is the one in charge of her happiness.

I have found several things that can effectively help me to be happier and more optimistic. One is to consciously think about it. Don't be too quick to call that idea way too simple—it might really work for you too.

How about writing down more of your experiences with tender mercies, with Heavenly help, with answered prayers, with protection and promptings and miracles? As I've done this (not perfectly, but a little more often recently), I have felt an increase in my depth of joy and gratitude.

One of the significant sources of help for me personally is the response I give to the question, "How are you?" Even if it seems more like a habit than a sincere question, I respond most of the time with "Happy!" Or "Happy, thank you." I've been doing that since I was about twenty-two and learned this response from Sister Florence Richards in the Missionary Home on North Main. It surprises and pleases me how many times that answer pushes and pulls me toward happiness.

How about letting a close friend or family member know that you want to be more optimistic and cheerful, and let them help you evaluate how you're doing. Part of this can be that they observe you, and part can be what you report to them.

As much as possible, spend more time with people who are happy. This is a challenge if you happen to live with Grumpy or a "sad sack," I know, but do your best to be around those who lift your spirits and help you to enjoy life.

Record your progress. Maybe you could carry a little notebook with you and write things in there from time to time: "I smiled at Richard." "I looked for beautiful things on my way to work and was surprised with how pretty the sunrise was; I think it had been a while since I'd noticed." "Instead of getting mad at my son for not practicing his tuba, as I usually do, I asked, 'How can I help?'" "This morning I put a rubber ducky and a cartoon in Grumpy's lunch bag."

You're not trying to become a stand-up comedian here—you're just trying to develop a more cheerful, positive nature. It can be done! Little by little and bit by bit, it can happen. Remember: happiness is a conscious choice!

We have more reasons to be happy than we could ever count. As Elder Neal A. Maxwell said: "Ultimate hope and daily grumpiness are not reconcilable. It is ungraceful, unjustified, and unbecoming of us as committed Church members to be constantly grumpy or of woeful countenance" (Thanksgiving speech, 26 November 1980).

Added to being cheerful is the ability to cultivate a good sense of humor, and the ability to laugh, especially at ourselves. President James E. Faust reminded: "Don't forget to laugh at the silly things that happen. Humor . . . is a powerful force for good when used with discretion. Its physical expression, laughter, is highly therapeutic" (*Church News,* 22 November 1997).

These are, of course, just a few ideas about cultivating qualities and characteristics related to being cheerful. I'll list just a few more qualities without much comment, thinking that perhaps you'll find one you'd like to work on.

I'll start with a rather long quote by President Gordon B. Hinckley. As you read this excerpt from a talk he gave to young women, notice how many times he invites them to cultivate an attribute, an art, a quality.

> You are loved by your Father in Heaven, of whose divine nature you have partaken. And He desires that His Holy Spirit will be near you wherever you go if you will invite it and *cultivate* it.
>
> There is something of divinity within each of you. You have such tremendous potential with that quality as a part of your inherited nature. Every one of you was endowed by your Father in Heaven with a tremendous capacity to do good in the world. Train your minds and your hands that you may be equipped to serve well in the society of which you are a part. *Cultivate* the art of being kind, of being

> thoughtful, of being helpful. Refine within you the quality of mercy which comes as a part of the divine attributes you have inherited.
>
> Some of you may feel that you are not as attractive and beautiful and glamorous as you would like to be. Rise above any such feelings, *cultivate* the light you have within you, and it will shine through as a radiant expression that will be seen by others.
>
> You need never feel inferior. You need never feel that you were born without talents or without opportunities to give them expression. *Cultivate* whatever talents you have, and they will grow and refine and become an expression of your true self appreciated by others ("The Light within You," *Ensign*, May 1995, 99; emphasis added).

Now, which of the following characteristics or qualities (or other attributes not listed below) would you most like to work on cultivating?

TESTIMONY

President Gordon B. Hinckley:

> With all of our doing, with all of our leading, with all of our teaching, the most important thing we can do for those whom we lead is to cultivate in their hearts a living, vital, vibrant testimony and knowledge of the Son of God, Jesus Christ, the Redeemer of the world, the Author of our salvation, He who

> atoned for the sins of the world and opened the way of salvation and eternal life. I would hope that in all we do we would somehow constantly nourish the testimony of our people concerning the Savior. I am satisfied—I know it's so—that whenever a man has a true witness in his heart of the living reality of the Lord Jesus Christ, all else will come together as it should. . . . That is the root from which all virtue springs among those who call themselves Latter-day Saints ("Inspirational Thoughts," *Ensign,* August 1997, 3).

Sometimes I've written down what I believe, and I find that instead of always putting "I know" I might put "I'm convinced that . . ." or "I believe deeply that . . ."

As Brian Price wrote in an article in the *New Era,* "I used to think that a testimony came suddenly, like a brilliant burst of the Spirit of the Holy Ghost in the heart. I never realized that a testimony could develop quietly and gently" ("Writing a Testimony," *New Era,* August 1997, 15).

GRATITUDE

President Gordon B. Hinckley:

"We should be thankful for the time in which we live. Cultivate a thankful heart" ("News of the Church," *Ensign,* June 1996, 74).

"Cultivate a spirit of thanksgiving for the blessing of life and for the marvelous gifts and privileges each of us enjoy" ("With

All Thy Getting Get Understanding," *Ensign*, August 1988, 3–4).

President James E. Faust:

> Carefully nurture every feeling of gratitude, no matter how small. Cultivating an attitude of gratitude is much like caring for the seed of faith. If we nourish the first tiny sprout, in time it will grow into a beautiful and fruitful tree (see Alma 32:27–37). I find that when I first become aware of a blessing, I can strengthen my feeling of gratitude if I immediately express my thanks. As with all commandments, gratitude is a description of a successful mode of living. The thankful heart opens our eyes to a multitude of blessings that continually surround us. . . . I hope that we may cultivate grateful hearts so that we may cherish the multitude of blessings that God has so graciously bestowed. May we openly express such gratitude to our Father in Heaven and our fellowmen ("Gratitude As a Saving Principle," *Ensign*, December 1996, 6).

I have found that my happiness depends in large part on the depth of my gratitude—my ability to feel and express thanks to God and others for the incredible blessings in my life.

We can cultivate gratitude by working to be more aware of the blessings that surround us. We can count our many blessings and name them one by one. Try that sometime—begin listing everything you can think of for which you are grateful, and

I think you'll find you begin thinking of things you hadn't thought of for a long, long time. That happened to me when I did this, and it was a sweet experience. You might even write down the list so you can refer back to it if you have times when you're not feeling too red-hot grateful.

We can cultivate gratitude by offering thank-you prayers to our Heavenly Father—prayers in which we don't ask for anything but rather focus on thanking Him. After a few minutes, such prayers go pretty deep and become powerful experiences.

We can also cultivate gratitude by thanking others. Can you think of someone you have wanted to thank, or whom you need to thank? Have the courage and the courtesy to say thank you. A phone call or a thank-you note can make such a difference not just for you but for the one you thank.

One specific thing I try to do that makes a huge difference is to think more often about what I DO have than what I DON'T have. When I'm focusing on what I don't have, I tend to become crabby and awful to be around. When I'm grateful—focusing on all that I have—it brings a sense of happiness, peace, and contentment, and an almost overwhelming feeling of gratitude.

THE GIFT OF THE HOLY GHOST

Elder Richard G. Scott: "With the gift of the Holy Ghost comes the ability to develop a powerfully sensitive capacity to make the right choices. Cultivate that gift. As the Lord has said, that is accomplished by consistent, righteous living. As you enhance your capacity to sense the direction of that infallible influence, you will avoid disappointment, discouragement, and even tragedy" ("He Lives," *Ensign,* November 1999, 87).

As we cultivate spirituality—learning how to seek, recognize, respond to, and enjoy the gift of the Holy Ghost—we become more like our Heavenly Father and the Savior.

Strengthening Families and Marriages

President Gordon B. Hinckley:

"In order to cultivate a strong nation, we must cultivate strong homes" ("News of the Church," *Ensign,* November 1996, 111).

"Let us continually work to strengthen our families. Let husbands and wives cultivate a spirit of absolute loyalty one to another. Let us not take one another for granted, but let us constantly work to nurture a spirit of love and respect for each other. We must guard against faultfinding, anger, and disrespect one for another" ("Thanks to the Lord for His Blessings," *Ensign,* May 1999, 88–89).

Friendship

President Gordon B. Hinckley: "Brothers and sisters, look above your trials. Try to forget your own pain as you work to alleviate the pain of others. Mingle together as opportunity affords. It is important that we do so. We need others to talk with and to share our feelings and faith with. Cultivate friends. Begin by being a good friend to others" ("A Conversation with Single Adults," *Ensign,* March 1997, 63).

Elder Robert D. Hales: "Cultivate good friends who do not try to make you choose between their ways and the Lord's ways. Be the kind of friend who makes it easier for others to obey the commandments when they are with you" ("If Thou Wilt Enter into Life, Keep the Commandments," *Ensign*, May 1996, 36).

I think people miss a lot when they don't take time to cultivate friendships!

REVERENCE

President Gordon B. Hinckley: "We need to strengthen our sacrament meetings and make them hours of worship in very deed. Cultivate a spirit of reverence, an attitude in which people come into the chapel and are quiet and reverent and thoughtful. There is too much noise. We are a social people, but I wish we would not keep it up so loudly in the chapel" ("Inspirational Thoughts," *Ensign*, August 1997, 6).

I guess that's more than enough to get us started on finding things to cultivate, isn't it? The list is almost endless—charity, courage, traditions, confidence, pondering, cooperation—on and on. Each of us as a child of our Heavenly Father has divine potential in ANY quality or attribute! We just need to cultivate these attributes throughout our lives.

Along with whatever "vital signs" we decide to work on, may we do our best just to do good and be good. Remember: Genuine Saints (as in Latter-day Saints) are those who are doing the best they can in their particular seasons of life.

HIGHLY RECOMMENDED READING

Joe J. Christensen, "Ten Ideas to Increase Your Spirituality," *Ensign*, March 1999, 58–61.

Joseph B. Wirthlin, "Cultivating Divine Attributes," *Ensign*, November 1998, 25–28.

Jack H. Goaslind, "Happiness," *Ensign*, May 1986, 52–54.

CHAPTER 6

Row, Row, Row Your Boat

I used to get a ton of things in the mail inviting me to send in a response that might make me a winner of a whole bunch of money. I saved one from Publisher's Clearing House years ago that had the following message on the huge envelope: "Don't throw away ten million dollars!"

I used to send in everything (almost) that came my way, and I would fantasize about how I'd spend my millions (the amount kept rising as years went by). Usually I'd write down first the tithing I would give, in case that would give me some Heavenly help in winning the contest. (Oh sure! As if!)

At some point I came to my senses (having won not a penny) and realized that I was spending way too much time and energy trying to get something for nothing.

Interestingly, I seldom get things like that in the mail

anymore. They seem to have lost interest in MEE, just as I've lost interest in them.

Perhaps you've heard some of the same reports I have about people who have "won" huge amounts of money—like millions of dollars for the winning lottery ticket—and then have expressed regret that it ever happened. Some have felt like their lives have been ruined. I've read of people who have filed fraudulent tax returns, struggled with substance abuse, served time in jail, dealt with lawsuits . . . their fairy tale turned into a nightmare! Their experiences took a terrible toll on family and other relationships, and many commented that the money had brought only misery and distress. One winner said he wished he'd torn up the ticket.

But do you ever feel like you want a chance to try? "It wouldn't ruin me!" "Show me the money!" "Let ME have this problem!"

I want to share a statement that helped me understand that there is NO SUCH THING as something for nothing. Never ever. It's from the First Presidency of the Church from October 1936: "Our primary purpose was to set up, in so far as it might be possible, a system under which the curse of idleness would be done away with, the evils of a dole abolished, and independence, industry, thrift, and self-respect be once more established amongst our people. The aim of the Church is to help the people to help themselves. Work is to be re-enthroned as the ruling principle of the lives of our Church membership" (Heber J. Grant, J. Reuben Clark Jr., David O. McKay, October 1936, as quoted in *Providing in the Lord's Way: A Leader's Guide to Welfare*

[Salt Lake City: The Church of Jesus Christ of Latter-day Saints, 1990], 6).

That is such a powerful statement. I'm thrilled by the idea that the Church helps us to help ourselves and then each other.

I could comment on almost every word and phrase, but for now I want to focus on the last sentence. Notice that work is to be re-enthroned as THE ruling principle, not just A ruling principle in the lives of Church members.

And indeed, as peculiar as it may seem to others OR to us, we "have work enough to do ere the sun goes down" (*Hymns,* no. 224)!

And what is the opposite of work? The dole and idleness, I suppose. It's thought-provoking to consider what the Brethren meant by "the CURSE of idleness" and "the EVILS of a dole."

In your experience, is this true? Do we try to win the lottery or the jackpot or the prize money so we don't have to work? Do we sometimes even cheat or lie?

And what is evil about getting something for nothing? Is it even evil to anticipate or expect or try to get something for nothing? Entitlements?

President Marion G. Romney used to share often the story of "The Gullible Gull." It seems that seagulls in a certain area learned to rely for their food on the scraps thrown them by boaters in a shrimp fleet. After several generations, the fleet moved on, and the gulls, who had never been taught to fish for themselves, starved to death. There was plenty of food available, but they didn't have the capacity to gather it because they had relied too long on something-for-nothing handouts.

The something-for-nothing habit is destructive, but perhaps not in the way that first comes to mind. The price the seagulls paid was much higher than their lives—it was their freedom, their agency.

It would have been peculiar, wouldn't it, if in the midst of all those "free-lunch" seagulls there had been some birdies who realized what was actually happening, and an observer could watch them each day teaching their little ones how to fish, continuing with their encouragement even though the baby and toddler birdies could see the "easy meals" happening not far away and might even have asked, "Why do we have to be different from our friends?"

What might the self-reliant seagulls have felt when they saw their neighbors and friends starving and dying? It might have been an "oil in the lamps" kind of experience.

Or perhaps the feelings might have been similar to those of Noah and his family as the floodwaters began to rise and there was no way to allow more people to board the ark. The time for choosing to get aboard had passed.

So why did I choose "Row, Row, Row Your Boat" as the title of this chapter? You've probably already figured it out. Increasingly it seems that we can't just sit in our boat and drift. The current that would carry us downstream is getting stronger and stronger. So is the encouragement and impression to ROW.

At this point in the history of everything, it's not "gently down the stream," as it was when the song was written. Now it feels more like we're needing to go UPSTREAM, and the current is getting stronger all the time. Don't just float, or you'll go over the falls!

As peculiar as it might seem, work is good for us. We were designed to work! The sense of satisfaction and accomplishment that comes from physical or mental work is vital to our growth, our happiness, our contentment.

Work, then, is one of the core ingredients of self-reliance. Sadly, there seems to be a decrease in the emphasis on and belief in the work ethic, and thus our feelings about self-reliance and working for what we receive become more peculiar.

I know several—even many—men and women who have made fortunes through their hard work and wise investing but have kept working. They seem to have caught on to what happens when we're idle, and they're trying to avoid that curse.

It isn't just about money. Work is soul food!

Sometimes people misunderstand what self-reliance means. For us as Church members, it is a description of our desire and willingness to work for what we receive. What it does NOT mean is that we feel we can reach a point where we are completely self-sufficient and don't need anyone else, including God.

Elder Dallin H. Oaks gave a warning about self-reliance leading to materialism if we're not wise and careful:

> Another strength that can become our downfall stems from self-reliance. We are told to be self-reliant, to provide for ourselves and those dependent upon us. But success at that effort can easily escalate into materialism. This happens through carrying the virtue of "providing for our own" to the point of

> excessive concern with accumulating the treasures of the earth. I believe this relationship identifies materialism as a peculiar Mormon weakness, a classic example of how Satan can persuade some to drive a legitimate strength to such excess that it becomes a disabling weakness ("Our Strengths Can Become Our Downfall," *Ensign,* October 1994, 18).

Keeping in mind what self-reliance really means, then, let's look at this important principle more closely.

President Thomas S. Monson has taught, "*Self-reliance* is a product of our work and under-girds all other welfare practices. It is an essential element in our spiritual as well as our temporal well-being" ("Guiding Principles of Personal and Family Welfare," *Ensign,* September 1986, 3).

President Marion G. Romney also tied work and self-reliance to spiritual growth when he said: "A dole is a dole whatever its source. All our Church and family actions should be directed toward making our children and members self-reliant. Let us work for what we need. Let us be self-reliant and independent. Salvation can be obtained on no other principle. Salvation is an individual matter, and we must work out our own salvation in temporal as well as in spiritual things" (Welfare Services Meeting Report, 2 October 1976, 13).

The Church of Jesus Christ of Latter-day Saints provides a positive way of life that affects members and families both spiritually and temporally.

President Gordon B. Hinckley reminded us that we need to work to get out of debt in order to be self-reliant: "We are carrying a message of self-reliance throughout the Church. Self-reliance cannot obtain when there is serious debt hanging over a household. One has neither independence nor freedom from bondage when he is obligated to others" ("To the Boys and to the Men," *Ensign,* November 1998, 53).

President J. Reuben Clark Jr. said: "The real long-term objective of the welfare plan is the building of character in the members of the Church, givers and receivers, rescuing all that is finest down deep inside of them, and bringing to flower and fruitage the latent richness of the spirit, which after all is the mission and purpose and reason for being of this Church" (*Providing in the Lord's Way,* inside front cover).

I love the idea of *rescuing* our finest feelings, no matter how deep inside of us they may be.

Self-reliance helps us as Church members to become prepared to care for ourselves and others, sharing generously with those in need. We are increasingly peculiar in our efforts to get out of debt and stay out of debt, to live within our means, save for planned expenses, avoid waste, care for our possessions, produce at least part of what we consume as we can, and carefully use our time.

"Heavenly Father never forsakes us, but he does not do for us what we can do for ourselves. He has commanded us to use the things we receive from him to take care of ourselves and our families. When we do so, we are self-reliant" (*Providing in the Lord's Way,* 5).

We also work to become educated, develop career skills, have a savings and insurance plan if possible, store a supply of food and other resources as we are able, maintain good health and fitness, and prepare for emergencies.

President Ezra Taft Benson quoted an old saying that fits well with regard to preparedness: "It is better to prepare and prevent than it is to repair and repent" ("News of the Church," *Ensign,* December 1987, 67).

The Lord asks us to be independent and self-reliant to the extent of our ability. A great part of the gospel program and welfare services is designed to help us increase the extent of our ability.

Think about how your own parents helped you to learn the value and importance of working for what you received. You may remember some specific things they did to help you understand that you couldn't ever get something for nothing. If you're like me, you may also remember that you weren't exactly thrilled about this part of life at first, especially if you had friends and classmates who didn't have to work the way you did.

I've asked many parents how they taught their children to work, and some have admitted that they didn't. They now regret the ways in which they spoiled their children by giving them something for nothing.

We've all heard the truth, "Give a man a fish, and you feed him for a day. Teach a man to fish, and you feed him for a lifetime." I used to tell missionaries to add another sentence: "Teach a man to teach others to fish, and store, and share, and you can go home."

When I was about fourteen years old I saw something in the window at Woods' store on Main Street that I really, really wanted: a pair of genuine Red Wing hiking boots. I skipped all the way home to tell Mom and Dad about them. They would be perfect for "field day" at school! They were only $14.25 (or something like that).

My parents' response wasn't quite what I had expected. "They sound wonderful. What can we do to help you earn the money?"

WHAT? How hard can it be for parents to give their precious little daughter enough money for some hiking boots?

But I realized they were serious, so I got to work. I was already doing quite a bit of baby-sitting, and I continued with that. I also began selling night crawlers. I made my own sign to nail on a tree in our front yard: "Fish Bait, 15 cents a dozen."

Uncle Arthur (not my real uncle, but everyone in our neighborhood was "uncle" or "aunt") would let me come over when he stuck some electric rod thing into the ground, and boy, would the night crawlers pop out of the ground! I popped a few times myself when I got too close.

I had boxes and dirt and wet gunny sacks to keep my worms happy and healthy. One day I got an idea and pulled some apart, and both halves lived! I doubled my profits with that one amazing discovery! I tried thirds, but that didn't work—the middle never survived.

Slowly but surely I reached my goal: $14.25. And I went to Woods' store and spent a lot of time before I spent my money. I tried the boots on. It felt great to pull those leather laces together. I walked around, looking in the mirror and pretending I was already at field day, imagining how excited everyone was to see my brand new Red Wing hiking boots.

I think maybe the guys at Woods' called my mother once or twice to see if she could come and get me. I guess I was taking quite a while.

Eventually I knew I had what I wanted. I went to the counter, and I exchanged not just my $14.25 but myself. There was something different about having worked so hard for something. I know you have had similar experiences and can relate to what I was feeling.

They wrapped the boots in tissue paper and put them in the official Red Wing box. Oh, my! I walked carefully all the few blocks home to First West, being careful not to get hit by a car or anything.

I wanted to wear the boots to church, but Mom put her foot down on that idea (kind of a pun there, huh?). I'd put them on for a while, then take them off, wipe them carefully, wrap them in the tissue paper, and put them back in the box.

And of course I did wear them for field day, and I wore them the two summers I worked at Zion National Park, and I wore them for every possible occasion.

As the years went by, some of my younger brothers and sisters used them, and even some nieces and nephews.

In 1981, I returned from a long trip in Southeast Asia (where I had had the first hospitalization of my life—in Taipei, Taiwan), and my mother told me she had a surprise for me. The hiking boots! She'd had them resoled and put new laces in, and they were all shined. That touched me so much!

I still have the boots. You see, they became a symbol between me and my parents of working for what I received.

Sometimes when I had a problem I didn't know how to solve, the experience with the hiking boots would come up. It would remind me that I needed to do all I could to solve the problem, and then my parents would help with what I couldn't figure out or know how to do.

I think if my parents had just purchased the boots for me—which they probably could have done—I would not even remember them.

As you remember some of your own experiences, share them with your children and others. Let them know how much you value the blessings that come from working. Be an example of this important aspect of the gospel.

King Benjamin reminded us of blessings that come when we are obedient: "And moreover, I would desire that ye should consider on the blessed and happy state of those that keep the commandments of God. For behold, they are blessed in all things, *both temporal and spiritual;* and if they hold out faithful to the end they are received into heaven, that thereby they may dwell with God in a state of never-ending happiness" (Mosiah 2:41; emphasis added).

President Joseph F. Smith shared this thought in a magazine article: "It has always been a cardinal teaching with the Latter-day Saints that a religion that has not the power to save people temporally and make them prosperous and happy here cannot be depended upon to save them spiritually and to exalt them in the life to come" (The Truth about Mormonism," *Out West*, September 1905, 242).

Our leaders have taught that welfare work, with principles

of self-reliance and service, should not be looked at as "just another program," but as a critical part of our Church membership. President Spencer W. Kimball said: "Isn't the plan beautiful? Don't you thrill to this part of the gospel that causes Zion to put on her beautiful garments? When viewed in this light, we can see that Welfare Services is not a program, but the essence of the gospel. *It is the gospel in action.* It is the crowning principle of a Christian life" ("Welfare Services: The Gospel in Action," *Ensign,* November 1977, 77).

And Elder Marion G. Romney taught:

> I believe, as President Clark has said, that through the welfare program the Church is attempting to abide by the second commandment, "Thou shalt love thy neighbor as thyself" (Matthew 22:39); that the Lord tried to bring his people to this condition through the United Order but was unable to do so and had to take the United Order from us; that the records will show that the reason was the selfishness and greed of the people; that had the people lived the United Order, we could have had a millennium then, a hundred years ago; that if we do not go forward with the welfare program and live it now, it will be because of our selfishness and greed, and the Lord will take the program away from us; and that in such case the members of the Church a hundred years from now will look back upon our day with the realization of the fact that we could have brought in a millennium if we had but lived this law (in Conference Report, April 1947, 126).

Before leaving this topic, I want to explain briefly something I have pondered as I've been reading and studying. We start out in life DEPENDENT. We need our parents and others to feed us, clothe us, and keep us safe. Gradually we begin to assert our INDEPENDENCE, and we become increasingly self-reliant. If we skip that step, ouch!

But then, as we learn more about the commandment to love one another as Christ has loved us, we become INTERDEPENDENT. This is a wonderful achievement, this interdependence. I need you, and you need me. Your strengths can help make up for my weaknesses, and vice versa.

Interdependence is a way to describe a Zion society.

So row—row, row, row your boat UPSTREAM. The Millennium is right around the corner ahead of us, and the falls are downstream.

HIGHLY RECOMMENDED READING

I highly recommend you read a talk given by President Marion G. Romney in October 1982 called "The Celestial Nature of Self-reliance" (reprinted in *Ensign,* November 1982, 91–93). Then you'll understand what I've been trying to share. (And you'll wonder why I didn't just put his talk in for this chapter!)

Boyd K. Packer, "Self-Reliance," *Ensign,* August 1975, 85–89.

"News of the Church: Conversation on Self-Reliance," *Ensign,* February 1996, 79–80.

L. Tom Perry, "If Ye Are Prepared Ye Shall Not Fear," *Ensign,* November 1995, 35–37.

CHAPTER 7

Can You Cook?

Is it peculiar anymore not to be able to cook? I know it would have been unheard of once, but now I wonder. I've been thinking lately about cooking. It's something you probably don't even think about because you're so good at it. You can't remember when you didn't know how to whip up something from scratch (not chicken feed . . . you know what I mean).

As for me, when did I stop cooking? Did I ever really start?

How hard can it be to follow a recipe and have something magical happen?

That depends on who's answering the question. I testify that good cooking is not passed through genes. It's not a natural thing, like breathing or drooling.

Mostly I look for things in the store that have a simple message: "Just add water." But I used to be able to cook. Not everything—nothing too fancy—but I even used to make bread for several years when I was a teenager. Not anymore. Now it's all I can do to get around to buying bread.

I admit there are times when the fact that I can't cook puts me in an exceedingly uncomfortable position. A few years ago our ward was doing a recipe book, and they wanted every woman in the ward to contribute at least one recipe. My response was that I didn't have one. They asked if I could borrow one from my mother, and I said no, that it didn't seem right somehow. They went away.

But they came back. The news was not good. Whoever didn't contribute to the recipe book would be in charge of putting it together the next time. What?

Would that be as highly motivating to YOU as it was to MEE? I worked HARD and came up with two recipes, which I will share right here and now (thus avoiding all the calls, letters, and e-mails that will flood Deseret Book from people scrambling to get copies).

TOAST

Make sure your toaster is plugged in.

(Make sure you HAVE a toaster.)

Make sure you have bread.

Put a slice in each slot (usually two).

For one slice, see toaster instructions.

If you've lost the instructions, call the 1–800 number.

Push down the knob thing.

Wait and watch.

If smoke starts to come out, or if you smell that certain burned-toast smell, chances are the toast is way too done. Scrape off the part you don't want to eat. If there's nothing left when you quit scraping, start over.

HARD-BOILED EGGS

Note: The reason they're called HARD-boiled eggs is because they're hard to do.

Select a sturdy, medium-sized saucepan.

Fill the pan approximately ⅔ full of clean tap water. (I know it's confusing to say FILL the pan and then cut it down to ⅔, but . . . do your best.)

Choose a burner on the stove (eenie meenie miney mo works).

Place the pan (the one with water in it) on the burner on the stove on the frog on the log in the bottom of the sea. Oh . . . I meant to stop at burner on the stove. Go back! Go back!

Add a teaspoon of vinegar (you heard me: vinegar) and a teaspoon of salt to the water in the pan on the burner on the stove. These two things make the eggs comfortable and keep them from getting stressed and cracked during the process.

Place the eggs in the water in the pan. You can choose either an odd or an even number of eggs—the process doesn't seem adversely affected by an odd number. Just make sure the number of eggs you choose fits in the pan, that all the eggs are covered with water, and that there's space between the top of the water and the top of the pan in case you actually do get the water boiling.

Turn the stove on high. As soon as the water boils, turn it down a bit but keep it boiling. For about 10 minutes.

Caution: Do NOT go outside to watch a sunset while the eggs are boiling. Bad decision. I tried this once, and it should never ever be done.

When time's up, take the pan off the burner (might want to use hot pads), carry it to the sink (the one in the kitchen, preferably), turn on cold water, and start cooling the eggs down.

Crack 'n' peel (sounds like the name of a new store or a new kind of musical instrument)—eggs are best eaten without the shells.

Note: The yellow part in the middle is NOT a seed . . . do not discard it (and do not plant it; you will NOT get an eggplant—I promise).

P.S. Turn off the stove.

I know you're going to be shocked when I tell you that my recipes made it into the book. You'll be REALLY shocked when I tell you that the hard-boiled egg recipe made it into TWO recipe books! Okay, the books weren't widely distributed, but hey . . .

Now that I'm on a roll, I think I'll include a seasonal recipe. This one hasn't made it anywhere, really. It's a recipe for Figgy

Pudding. There probably IS an actual recipe for Figgy Pudding, but I've never seen one, so I made up my own. It is particularly astonishing that I could come up with a recipe for something I've never tasted. Maybe I got the idea from a box of figgies when I was in junior high.

An alternate name for the pudding is Piggy Pudding, in honor of my pig Fei (rhymes with "hey"), whom I met in Taiwan at Christmastime in 1962 while I was on a mission. Fei is once again letting us have copies of an "old family recipe," one that has made "hogs" of many of us through the years.

Here we go!

Figgy (Piggy) Pudding

4 cans (No. 2) figgies in light syrup

3 hard-boiled figgies, unpeeled (see hard-boiled egg recipe for some tips)

2 dozen diced figgies (not the same as the dice in your Parcheesi game)

2 dozen sliced figgies

7 kippered figgies (these are delicious! Try not to eat them all before you get a chance to see how they spiff up this recipe)

4 pints figgy juice (remember, color has nothing to do with taste)

4 small cans figgy juice concentrate (don't be fooled by substitutes)

1 Tbsp. figgy extract (I know it's expensive, but don't cheat on this ingredient)

1 Tbsp. extra-blend figgy oil

3 family-size boxes chocolate-covered figgies

DIRECTIONS:

Remove the chocolate from the chocolate-covered figgies and mix all the ingredients together. Boil to a lumpy consistency. Now remove all of the diced figgies from the mixture, being careful not to remove the sliced ones.

Toss what remains into a large vat (if you don't have a large enough vat, just use your bathtub). Swish it around (in any way you can manage).

Let it solidify (and it really WILL solidify).

Saw it into pieces (a chain saw works best)

Serve to as many as can handle it.

(Caution: This might reverse any tooth-whitening procedure and other dental magic that anyone in your party has undergone.)

Good luck.

Now you realize that I'm not just a "flash in the pan"! I have more than only TWO recipes. Isn't this impressive?

But there's so much I don't know about cooking. There's so much I've forgotten, and even more that I never really learned. Maybe it's this way because I live alone. When I had roommates, or when I was still at home, I was more motivated to cook.

It makes me nervous to be asked to help when I'm invited to dinner or a luncheon or a party. I always volunteer to set the table, entertain the kids, count chairs, or call the pizza hot line.

Think about something that's hard for you. Do you ever end up laughing about it, or does it make you so frightened or uncomfortable that you avoid any chance of anyone finding out or putting you on the spot?

A dear friend once told me she was called on to lead the singing in a meeting. She was terrified! Although she'd had many different callings in the Church, this was something she had never ever done, and she hadn't the slightest idea how to do it. She got help, and it worked out, but others were very surprised that she didn't know how.

Is it praying in a group that's hard for you? Is it giving a talk? Jogging? Reading? Sharing your testimony? Dancing? Talking to a stranger? Driving? Playing sports? Teaching a lesson? Swimming? Apologizing? Climbing trees? Writing? Talking to a child? Blowing bubbles? Doing missionary work? Fixing a leaky faucet? Doing the hula? Whistling? Being in a crowd?

We don't all have to know the very same things.

Think about how nice it is when those who know are willing to help those who don't know, when those who have are willing to share with those who don't have. Think of what you know and have, and how nice it is when you're the one willing to help those who don't know or have.

I think it's rather peculiar for someone to be concerned with and desirous of sharing. It seems such a common, "natural man" thing to want to hoard a skill, a recipe, a video game, a mountain bike, an idea.

My neighbor Shirley isn't that way at all. She loves sharing. She has taught more than 500 people to play the piano! I've watched through the years as cars have driven up to her home and little ones have hopped out for their lessons, books tucked under their arms.

I've asked Shirley if she has any students among those 500-plus who can play the piano better than she can now. She gave me the "DUH" look. Of course!

So I asked her if that was hard. And her answer: "Of course not!"

You see, she is peculiar. She loves having others learn and then "take off." There is no jealousy, no regret, no competition. What a way to live!

Read again the wonderful instruction from Doctrine and Covenants 82:17–19:

> And you are to be equal, or in other words, you are to have equal claims on the properties, for the benefit of managing the concerns of your stewardship, every man according to his wants and his needs, inasmuch as his wants are just—And all this for the benefit of the church of the living God, that every man may improve upon his talent, that every man may gain other talents, yea, even an hundred fold, to be cast into the Lord's storehouse, to become the common property of the whole church—Every man seeking the interest of his neighbor, and doing all things with an eye single to the glory of God.

So we gain talents and magnify them in order that we might be of use to God's children. We don't do it to show off.

A fellow I know named Don received an incredible

assignment to organize a huge event. He called Steve, his young and energetic friend, to work with him. He said, "WE have a new job." As time went on, Steve was somewhat more in the forefront, more visible, and an observer asked Don if this made him feel bad. "Oh no!" he responded. "I feel like Lehi . . . so proud of Nephi!"

What a wonderful way to feel! It makes sense, since all of our gifts and talents come from God in the first place, that we would use them to serve Him and His children.

Now let me approach it in another way. I'll ask if you can do some things, and you just nod your head (or, if you're in a public place, just think "yes" for the things you can do; I don't want you to embarrass yourself).

Can you:

Bake bread?

Change a car tire?

Fly a plane?

Use a computer?

Milk a cow?

Speak another language? (You can count Pig Latin).

Make homemade ice cream?

Read to a child?

Do a cartwheel?

Pick out a good watermelon?

Change a diaper?

Train a dog?

Find your way to the post office?

Sew a coat or suit?

Make cabinets?

Paint?

Play hopscotch?

Remember the name of your teacher from first grade?

Fly a kite?

Handle bees?

Rock climb?

Do CPR?

Fish?

Quilt?

Understand football?

Understand opera?

Plant a garden?

Do origami paper folding?

Write a letter?

Play a musical instrument?

Plan a family reunion?

The list is getting a bit long, but I hope I have enough variety in it that you and everyone reading can answer "yes" (or nod your head) at least once or twice.

What's the point? The point is, we don't all know how to do the same things. We don't all know and understand the same information.

This is what makes life so interesting and wonderful—we're not exactly like anyone else. We really do need each other.

So can you cook? If you're like me and it's not one of your strengths, isn't it wonderful to know there are many others who CAN cook? Yum!

HIGHLY RECOMMENDED READING

Anything by Betty Crocker.

John Thompson piano books.

Stephanie Ashcraft's books on 100 ways to use a taco, a cake mix, a potato, and so on. (Watch for the new book on grits.) I'm waiting for the one on 100 ways to consume chocolate! Go, Stephanie, go!

CHAPTER 8

Extreme Makeovers

Have you noticed how much excitement there is in our world lately about makeovers? Just about anything can be dramatically changed: a face, a fence, a kitchen, a whole home, a whole body, a basement, a yard, a day, an old pickup, a dress, a dog, an attitude.

Extreme makeovers have become pretty popular, especially on TV. There are contests to lose weight, or someone's home is remodeled, or someone gets a new hairdo and a lot of dental work, plus a fancy wardrobe. I remember seeing a woman on TV once who'd had so many plastic surgeries on her nose that she could no longer breathe through it!

I GOOGLED this phrase, "extreme makeover," and got half a million hits! Wow!

The web sites offer all kinds of information, including how

to sign up for a transformation, news about plastic surgeons and cosmetic dentists, and a whole gallery of before-and-after pictures. Many of those pictures are pretty dramatic. With some of them I notice that in the "before" picture the person isn't smiling or standing up straight. That increases the difference in the two pictures for sure.

I took a look at an application for a makeover. Whoa. You make a three-minute video, and then they ask you to go from head to toe, explaining what you would like changed. "List everything you would like to have altered."

The application has questions such as, "How will this change your life?" and, "Besides altering your appearance, what is your biggest dream?"

What is it we're looking for when we think of an extreme makeover?

What's missing?

I'd like to describe an extreme makeover that I feel answers those questions. It brings what is missing not just to our outside "look" but to our heart and our soul. It's a makeover that causes people to clap their hands and shout for joy, just as friends and family do in the many "extreme makeover" programs and contests. In this case the changes and joy are long-lasting—they can be eternal!

You likely know someone who has experienced this type of a makeover. Maybe it's YOU. I'm persuaded that it's a lot more dramatic than anything you'd ever see in a magazine or a movie or on TV.

Many makeovers of the type I'm thinking of are described

in scriptures. Ah . . . now you're catching on, if you hadn't already.

I'll begin my description by mentioning two different accounts of the birth of the Savior in the New Testament. The account in Luke 2:1–20 is likely the one we're more familiar with. We quote it each Christmastime, and many memorable family pageants are based on these beautiful verses.

The account in Matthew 2:1–12 tells of wise men from the East who came to Jerusalem searching for the Christ child. They asked others along the way if they knew where the King of the Jews was.

King Herod heard about this and was troubled. He called the wise men to him and found out when the star had appeared. He asked them to go search diligently and to let him know when they found the child, ostensibly so that he could go worship Him too. (You can tell I'm aware he had absolutely no plan to worship Jesus but instead wanted to destroy Him.)

The wise men continued following the star, rejoicing, and found Jesus. They worshiped Him and presented Him with gifts. They were then warned by God in a dream that they should not go back to Herod, and "they departed into their own country *another way.*"

I put the italics there because that phrase feels so significant. Once the wise men had found Jesus and had fallen down and worshiped Him and presented Him with gifts, they were changed. The warning to go home another way came from God so that Herod could not find the little King of the Jews, but the wise men likely went home changed in other ways as well.

My feeling is that the same thing can happen to us. WE can come close to the Savior, worship Him, and present Him with gifts (such as our love, obedience, reverence, our broken hearts and contrite spirits, and our determination to come unto Him, to follow Him). And we can be changed—we can be caused to go another way.

That is the essence of the extreme makeover I'm talking about. It begins inside. We call it a mighty change of heart.

There are many powerful examples of just such things happening in the scriptures. We read of what happened to Saul on the road to Damascus in the New Testament, of Alma Junior and the sons of Mosiah (and many others, including thousands of Lamanites at a time) in the Book of Mormon.

One of my favorite descriptions of these extreme makeovers is in the book of Mosiah. King Benjamin had just finished his remarkable message and wanted to know if his people had understood and believed what he had shared.

> And now, it came to pass that when king Benjamin had thus spoken to his people, he sent among them, desiring to know of his people if they believed the words which he had spoken unto them.
>
> And they all cried with one voice, saying: Yea, we believe all the words which thou hast spoken unto us; and also, we know of their surety and truth, because of the Spirit of the Lord Omnipotent, which has wrought a mighty change in us, or in our hearts, that we have no more disposition to do evil, but to do good continually (Mosiah 5:1–2).

This was no temporary, cosmetic, superficial kind of change (and yet I'll bet we could notice something if we had "before and after" pictures).

Two specific changes are noted. First, the people had no more disposition to do evil. But it was more than that. Their new hearts brought a disposition to do good continually. They felt more than just a desire to stop doing things that were wrong. They wanted to REPLACE their bad habits and less-than-perfect ways of living with doing good and being good. No wonder it's called a mighty change of heart!

Stopping doing wrong things would probably make someone "pretty good," but adding to that a desire to do good continually would bring them to a point of "striving to be even better."

I like the way President Ezra Taft Benson expressed the difference between a mighty change of heart and just a change of habit or routine.

> Repentance means more than simply a reformation of behavior. Many men and women in the world demonstrate great will-power and self-discipline in overcoming bad habits. . . . Such changes of behavior, even if in a positive direction, do not constitute true repentance. Repentance involves not just a change of actions, but a change of heart.
>
> When we have undergone this mighty change, which is brought about only through faith in Jesus Christ and through the operation of the Spirit upon us, it is as though we have become a new person.

> Thus the change is likened to a new birth. Thousands of you within the sound of my voice have experienced this change. You have forsaken lives of sin . . . and have become clean. You have no more disposition to return to your old ways. You are in reality a new person. This is what is meant by a change of heart ("A Mighty Change of Heart," *Ensign*, October 1989, 4).

In 1991 I met a wonderful woman named Betty who was just returning to the fold after having been gone for fifty years. In a letter to me, she explained that she had been "wandering in the wilderness, in absolute misery, for so many, many years."

She told me a lot about her life, and about her remarkable return. And then she wrote: "I am aware of that 'other' Betty disappearing and the 'new' Betty emerging." Wow! She got it! She really understood what was happening to her! A few years later we had the privilege of going to the Salt Lake Temple together, and she further described the wonderful changes that had come. She really did have a new heart!

This is REAL. These changes are deep and incredible. In fact, they may actually be a *returning* rather than something brand new. Perhaps this kind of makeover, this kind of change of heart, is a *becoming* experience. Maybe we're becoming who we really ARE, and who we have always BEEN.

There is a thought-provoking definition of repentance in the Bible Dictionary, back near the Topical Guide in your Bible (I've called it the "Tropical Guide" so often that I have trouble writing or saying it correctly). It says:

> The Greek word of which this [*repentance*] is the translation denotes a change of mind, i.e., a fresh view about God, about oneself, and about the world. Since we are born into conditions of mortality, repentance comes to mean a turning of the heart and will to God, a renunciation of sin to which we are naturally inclined. Without this there can be no progress in the things of the soul's salvation. . . . [We] must be cleansed in order to enter the kingdom of heaven. Repentance is not optional for salvation; it is a commandment of God (Bible Dictionary, 760).

I like that a lot! A change of mind! A fresh view about God, ourselves, and the world. Turning our hearts and will to God, and turning our backs on sin.

Without striving to be better even when we're already pretty good, we may stop progressing. We may block the process of turning our hearts and wills to God, a process that is so critical to the salvation of our souls.

We all need to make some changes in our lives, to do some turning and returning. There are times when we need to change both our minds and our hearts, our direction and our circumstances.

One of the visible changes that comes from this kind of extreme makeover, this change of heart, is a person's countenance. Such a mighty inner change cannot help but show on the outside.

Have you watched this in yourself or someone else? I remember one young man who had made a dramatic change after ten years of wandering in his own wilderness. He had made a complete return, and he had just received his patriarchal blessing prior to going on a mission.

When he walked into the room there was a visible change in his countenance. I could see it immediately. All the lights were on!

I went to him, put my hands on his shoulders, and asked, "Who are you?" Looking me straight in the eyes with incredible happiness and peace, he said so sweetly and joyfully, "I am a child of God!"

Few things in life are more thrilling than these kinds of experiences!

When we choose to follow Christ, to give Him our hearts and to make His will our will, we choose to be changed. "No man," said President David O. McKay, "can sincerely resolve to apply in his daily life the teachings of Jesus of Nazareth without sensing a change in his own nature. The phrase 'born again' has a deeper significance than many people attach to it. This changed feeling may be indescribable, but it is real" (in Conference Report, April 1962, 7).

President Marion G. Romney helped me consider more deeply the questions asked by Alma in the Book of Mormon:

> No one can read Alma's resumé of the experiences of his father with the saints who joined the church at the waters of Mormon; of the Lord's mercy and long-suffering in bringing them out of their spiritual and temporal captivity; of how by the power of the Holy Spirit, they were awakened from their deep sleep of

death to experience a mighty change wrought in their hearts—no one, I say, can contemplate this marvelous transformation without yearning to have a like change wrought in his own heart.

And no one can answer for himself these questions, which Alma put to his brethren:

"[1] . . . have ye spiritually been born of God? [2] Have ye received his image in your countenances? [3] Have ye experienced this mighty change in your hearts?

"[4] Do ye exercise faith in the redemption of him who created you? [5] Do you look forward with an eye of faith, and view this mortal body raised in immortality, and this corruption raised in incorruption, to stand before God to be judged according to the deeds which have been done in the mortal body?

"I say unto you, can you imagine to yourselves that ye hear the voice of the Lord, saying unto you, in that day: Come unto me ye blessed, for behold, your works have been the works of righteousness upon the face of the earth?

"[6] Have ye walked, keeping yourselves blameless before God? [7] Could ye say, if ye were called to die at this time . . . that ye have been sufficiently humble? That your garments have been cleansed and made white through the blood of Christ . . . ?" (Alma 5:14–16, 27.)

I say, no one with the spirit of the Book of

> Mormon upon him can honestly answer to himself these soul-searching questions without resolving to so live that he can answer them in the affirmative on that great day to which each of us shall come ("The Keystone of Our Religion," *Improvement Era,* December 1970, 53–54).

Can you think of some changes you'd like to make in your life? Most of us can, I'm sure. It means everything to me to know that it's possible—that with Heavenly help I really CAN make changes. Little ones, big ones, and even, as needed, EXTREME ones!

More than just a new nose, whitened teeth, and nice clothing, an extreme makeover of the kind I'm talking about brings peace of heart, peace of soul, a quiet and serene conscience, a sense of contentment and pure joy. And it lasts and lasts and lasts—all the way Home.

The Lord Himself asks this interesting question: "Whoso having knowledge, have I not commanded to repent?" (D&C 29:49).

My friend Susan was concluding an interview with her stake president to renew her temple recommend several years ago. He had asked her all the questions, and the recommend had been signed. Then, as she was leaving, he added something else: "Susan, think of the worst thing you're doing." Almost without a pause he then asked, "Have you got it?"

She said of course she had it! Instantly! Then he said, "Quit it! And when you've quit that, then start on the next thing, and then the next." A profoundly thought-provoking experience!

I used to think of repentance as an annual thing. You go to the bishop once a year with a list and your Kleenex, and you pour out all that's on your mind, and he says, "Go thy way and sin no more," and you begin saving up again for the next year.

Repentance is not just an event, is it—it's a process. A mighty change of heart begins with a deep personal desire to change, to become clean, to return. There have been times when such a change has seemingly occurred in one spectacular EVENT—such as for the Apostle Paul, and for Alma Jr.—but for most of us it seems to be a daily, continuing striving a little harder to be a little better.

One Sunday after I had taught a lesson to a group of missionaries at the Missionary Training Center, I noticed an elder waiting to talk to me. He told me he needed to write me a letter, and I gave him my MTC address.

A while later I received an incredible account of his efforts to prepare himself to be a representative of Jesus Christ. With his permission I'm going to share part of that long, wonderful letter.

> To put it best, my years before my mission weren't the greatest, to say the least. I really didn't have an eternal perspective on life, which led me to do many things that caused a lot of hurting later.
>
> I liked what President Packer had to say about changing behavior: "Doctrine can change behavior quicker than talking about behavior." So it was for me.
>
> I had a very special Book of Mormon teacher. I

> rarely missed a class . . . he was so special. Probably by the time the year was over I read the Book of Mormon 3–4 times. It was alive, and full of beautiful conversations and pure doctrine, and many admonitions as to what will happen to those who don't repent.
>
> I can remember many sleepless nights, hours and hours on my knees crying, an awful misery living with guilt and godly sorrow for my sins. Oh, how many times I thought all was lost and there was no hope. I went through my freshman year with a superficial smile, wanting so bad to be "clean and whole" again.
>
> I read *The Miracle of Forgiveness* for the 2nd or 3rd time, which harrowed me up by the memory of my sins to the Nth degree. I was ready.
>
> I can remember how difficult it was to speak to [my bishop back home], to say the words. But how wonderful I felt afterwards. By some miracle my sinful burdens were lifted. . . . [I] went through a good and marvelous purifying process, even writing elementary teachers and confessing that I had cheated on a test . . . and many other acts of restitution that were a lot harder than that. . . . But oh the joy with each little act to put me back on the straight and narrow.

This young man pleaded with Heavenly Father to know that he had been forgiven. He received a strong impression to visit his Book of Mormon teacher, and through amazing non-coincidences, he found him in his office and was able to receive a wonderful priesthood blessing from him. Among other things, he remembers that his teacher said the following in this blessing: "A great burden has been taken from your shoulders and laid at the altar at the feet of Jesus Christ. Your heart is in the right place. Look not to the past, only to the present and the future."

And then this young man finished his long letter to me: "How grateful I am for my Lord and Savior Jesus Christ and His atoning sacrifice. May I just say, I know what extra heavy baggage is . . . but I also know what it's like at the altar, at the feet of Jesus Christ. Thank you for this opportunity to remind me of my personal conversion and my Savior. I hope in some way you can help others with my experience."

Maybe you can imagine how deeply I was touched by this young man's letter and testimony. He reminded me of so many important things. It was so remarkable that he even wrote to elementary school teachers to ask their forgiveness!

I'm convinced that as we make changes in our lives and receive the gift of forgiveness, it causes us to reach out to others as we never have before with increased kindness and with sweet forgiving. "Blessed are the merciful: for they shall obtain mercy" (Matthew 5:7).

One day at the MTC I saw something bright orange lying on the floor. As I got closer I realized it was right at the bottom of a painting of the Savior—right at His feet. It was a huge duffel bag, and it had a big tag on it that read: "Extra heavy baggage."

I couldn't quit looking at it—what an amazing picture! Someone had literally dropped their extra heavy baggage at the feet of the One who could help carry it!

> *Cast thy burden upon the Lord,*
> *And he shall sustain thee.*
> *He never will suffer the righteous to fall.*
> *He is at thy right hand.*
> *Thy mercy, Lord, is great*
> *And far above the heav'ns.*
> *Let none be made ashamed*
> *That wait upon thee.*
> (Hymns, *no. 110)*

I was thinking in sacrament meeting one Sunday morning about how important it is that we help each other through these spiritual extreme makeovers—especially that we help those with the heaviest of burdens: sin.

My thought was that sometimes we're not very helpful. Seeing someone in the hall after a long absence, we might make comments like, "Wow! Stand clear! Don's back, and I think the roof's going to fall in!" What kind of a welcome is that?

When others have decided to come back, we should be like the father was with the returning prodigal son—we should run to meet them! Our welcome, support, and encouragement should be genuinely kind and Christlike.

I know Jesus Christ is our Savior and Redeemer. I am convinced that the more we strive to become like Him, the more we will want to change, to return, to repent. We really WILL have a fresh view about God and ourselves and the world and people around us.

The Savior has been sent to heal and to save, to lift and bless those who are crushed by the weight of their sins, to comfort those who are lonely and in despair, to bind up the broken-hearted, and to give peace.

Let's come unto Christ with all our hearts and help others to come unto Him as well, that He may heal us, save us, and bring us safely Home.

Highly Recommended Reading

Ezra Taft Benson, "Born of God," *Ensign*, November 1985, 5–7.

Alexander B. Morrison, "For This Cause Came I into the World," *Ensign*, November 1999, 25–27.

CHAPTER 9

Carpenter Seed

On the road between my home and my work, there's a little store with a name that I love: Carpenter Seed. I've driven by it thousands of times in both directions. And I've been inside many times.

When I walk in, my attention is immediately captured by the entire south wall full of seed packets with bright, colorful pictures on them. Tomatoes, marigolds, peas, beans, pumpkins, melons, petunias, carrots, radishes, sweet peas, squash . . . and a whole bunch of varieties of each thing.

The pictures are so colorful and perfect. How DO they get the veggies, flowers, and fruits to hold so still and be so pretty? I don't know if the pictures have been touched up or not, but whoever took them did a great job. They got 'em on their best day.

It is amazing to me—awesome, really—that each package

contains seeds that were meant to become what's in the picture on the package. (I don't think results are guaranteed.)

There is a big difference between going into Carpenter Seed and another kind of store—say, a Piggly Wiggly, Albertsons, Safeway, Ralphs, or farmer's market. When we buy the finished product, either fresh or frozen, canned or ready-to-eat, we have been able to skip a whole lot of steps. Someone else took those steps for us. They prepared the ground, planted the seeds, added water, did the weeding, prayed for sunshine, and gathered the harvest.

I remember Jim and Joe Carnesecca in the orchards that used to be across the street from us in Mapleton, and how HARD they worked to care for and protect the growing fruit in anticipation of a good harvest. I remember many times when there would be a change in the weather, and they'd burn a bunch of "smudge pots" to try to keep the fruit from freezing.

But when we go to Carpenter Seed, we apparently have decided (or have been talked into it) to participate in all the steps, and we get to learn a lot of important lessons about "the law of the harvest" (patience, long-suffering, endurance, and so on). Oh joy!

Seeds don't often look much like what's going to grow, do they? Have you noticed that? Most of the time the seeds are disguised, so you really can't tell what they're going to be unless you keep them in the package.

Carrot seeds have long intrigued me. They look like little specks of dirt. They're not the color or shape of carrots in any way. But inside of them, that's what they are: carrots! I can't plant carrots and pray for corn or a tomato. Well, I guess I could, but I know you get my meaning.

That's that. That's just the way it is. If I want a melon, I plant the seed that will grow up to be a melon. I'll never get a pumpkin from a seed that was meant to be a bean, or a pink flower from something that is meant to be a radish.

What does this have to do with being peculiar?

Let's suppose that Carpenter Seed is Jesus' store. He was a carpenter, as you know, and that's probably one reason I love the name of the store so much. So let's suppose it's the Carpenter's Seed store.

You walk in, and on that whole south wall are, as we expected, packets of seeds. Only this time they're for qualities, gospel principles, gifts, characteristics we want to develop. There are WORDS we can plant, not in the soil of the earth, but in our hearts.

Maybe the packages say things like "charity," "integrity," "compassion," "knowledge," "obedience," "an understanding heart," "patience," and so on.

In this case there is no Piggly Wiggly. No drive-through with "service on a stick," "kindness to go," or "new and improved obedience, half off, today only," "charity in 10 minutes or your money back." These qualities, skills, talents, or whatever we want to call them must be planted in our hearts and helped to grow and develop.

Think of Alma 32, the chapter in the Book of Mormon where Alma Junior teaches about planting words in our hearts and helping them grow. I'll say more about this in a few pages.

For now I just want to remind us that we must prepare a place in our hearts for these seeds, these words, to be planted, and we must help them take root.

Suppose I don't plant anything. What happens? Think of a garden spot (or anywhere in a yard or field). What happens when "nothing" is planted? Is it "nothing" that grows? No. It's WEEDS! Noxious weeds!

I remember one weed in particular that grew in my yard one year. When it was just a little feller I could have plucked it out of the ground so easily, with just a thumb and a finger, pinching it right out of my yard and my life! But I didn't. I let it grow. I wanted to see what would happen.

It got so huge that I was thinking of entering it in the county or state fair. It kept growing taller and stronger. It got taller than I was. Somewhere in my basement I have a picture of me with my weed. It had to be at least 6 feet tall (but I had a hard time getting it to stand straight for the photo; it seemed kind of awkward and self-conscious).

Eventually I had to kill it. It was like cutting down Jack's bean stalk! The unseen root system must have gone all over the neighborhood for blocks and blocks! It took me quite a while to chop and saw that huge weed into garbage-can-sized pieces. That became a powerful analogy to me about getting rid of sin early and planting good things in our lives instead.

We can't just HOPE good things will come to us. We can't expect wonderful qualities of character and heart without any effort. If we want Godlike and Christlike attributes—if it is our plan and desire to become more like They are—we must plant good seeds. On purpose. Consciously. Carefully.

Let me approach all of this another way. I love sports. I find I don't spend as much time watching and participating in sports as I used to, but for many years that was a big part of my life.

I remember watching a lot of basketball and football games with my dad. I started out listening on the radio, and I would draw pictures of what I thought the "4 B's" from the U of U looked like. I can no longer remember the names of all four, but it was something like Buckwalter, Bunte, Bergen . . . well, I used to be able to name them easily, but now they're stored too far from the surface of my brain and out of reach of my not-so-hot retrieval system.

For around twenty years I subscribed to *Sports Illustrated*, and I probably spent more time with that magazine than I did with any other. My mother even sent my copies to me while I was a missionary in Indonesia, and I'm convinced that increased my popularity with the elders. Ha ha ha.

I enjoy watching many different sports and sporting events. I get pretty excited when it's time for the Olympics. I have thought it would be a great thrill to participate, and especially to win a medal.

Several years ago I began paying attention to all the preparations being made to hold the games in Greece. It seemed to me it was a special thing to have the Olympic Games return to their place of origin.

So I started dreaming about joining up. Maybe I could sign up for a few events. Just pick something that's not too hard and call someone up to see if there's a spot. Oh, sure!

It sounds stupid, doesn't it? I meant for it to sound stupid. We all know that athletes prepare for YEARS, not just for a few hours or days, to even make it to the Olympic Games. And throughout all those years of exercising and training, there were not many cheering crowds and banners and all. MOST of the preparation was done behind the scenes, so to speak. Some of the athletes have literally had participating in the Olympics as a goal since they were "knee-high to a grasshopper."

As silly as it is to imagine that we could leap in to the Olympics at the last minute, isn't it just as ridiculous to suppose that we can grow spiritually and purify our thoughts in a short time, without much effort? We readily recognize the need to work hard for physical fitness, well-being, and performance—wouldn't the same principles hold true for spiritual fitness? Oh, if only we spent as much time and concern on our spiritual diets and fitness as we do on our physical diets and fitness! (I have to admit here that I need a lot of work on BOTH.)

Elder Joseph B. Wirthlin taught this well: "To soundly plant good seeds in your heart requires prolonged, intense, unremitting pondering. It is a deep, ongoing, regenerating process which refines the soul" ("Pondering Strengthens the Spiritual Life," *Ensign*, May 1982, 24).

Now back to Alma chapter 32 in the Book of Mormon. Alma Junior and his outstanding team of missionaries had gone to preach to the Zoramites, a group of apostates who had become really confused about how to worship.

Alma 31:5 tells of the preparation Alma and his missionary companions made: "And now, as the preaching of the word had a great tendency to lead the people to do that which was just—yea, it had had more powerful effect upon the minds of the people than the sword, or anything else, which had happened unto them—therefore Alma thought it was expedient that they should try the virtue of the word of God."

The planting and nourishing of gospel principles in the heart and soul is a conscious effort. It doesn't "just happen." It involves diligently searching the scriptures and the words of the living prophets and then nourishing them (including applying what we learn). As Alma put it:

> Now, we will compare the word unto a seed. Now, if ye give place, that a seed may be planted in your heart, behold, if it be a true seed, or a good seed, if ye do not cast it out by your unbelief, that ye will resist the Spirit of the Lord, behold, it will begin to swell within your breasts; and when you feel these swelling motions, ye will begin to say within yourselves—It must needs be that this is a good seed, or that the word is good, for it beginneth to enlarge my soul; yea, it beginneth to enlighten my understanding, yea, it beginneth to be delicious to me.
>
> Now behold, would not this increase your faith? I say unto you, Yea (Alma 32:28–29).

Just as soil needs preparation for a seed, so does a human heart for the word of God to take root. Before he told the people to plant the seed, Alma told them that their hearts had been prepared. Either by choice or by persecution, they had become HUMBLE.

Once they are planted in our hearts, how do we NOURISH

those good words? Alma gives a formula for nourishing the word and helping it grow:

> And behold, as the tree beginneth to grow, ye will say: Let us nourish it with great care, that it may get root, that it may grow up, and bring forth fruit unto us. And now behold, if ye nourish it with much care it will get root, and grow up, and bring forth fruit.
>
> But if ye neglect the tree, and take no thought for its nourishment, behold it will not get any root; and when the heat of the sun cometh and scorcheth it, because it hath no root it withers away, and ye pluck it up and cast it out.
>
> Now, this is not because the seed was not good, neither is it because the fruit thereof would not be desirable; but it is because your ground is barren, and ye will not nourish the tree, therefore ye cannot have the fruit thereof.
>
> And thus, if ye will not nourish the word, looking forward with an eye of faith to the fruit thereof, ye can never pluck of the fruit of the tree of life.
>
> But if ye will nourish the word, yea, nourish the tree as it beginneth to grow, by your faith with great diligence, and with patience, looking forward to the fruit thereof, it shall take root; and behold it shall be a tree springing up unto everlasting life (Alma 32:37–41).

The words (seeds) that we plant in our hearts need to be nurtured with great care. Let's say I have chosen a seed called "charity." I prepare a place in my heart to plant this sweet seed.

Preparing a place in my heart would likely include having an earnest desire to become more charitable. It might include a consciousness of the gap between what my heart tells me and what I sometimes think or say or do so impulsively.

Another way I could prepare to plant this seed, and then help it to grow and fill my heart, would be to pray for Heavenly help. As Mormon taught, "pray unto the Father with all the energy of heart, that ye may be filled with this love, which he hath bestowed upon all who are true followers of his Son, Jesus Christ" (Moroni 7:48).

I'm convinced we actually CAN develop wonderful, Godlike and Christlike qualities in our lives no matter what our home life or other circumstances have been. We are children of God, and we have the potential to become like Him! And even when we realize we're not perfect—even when we're striving but feel like we're slipping—the potential is still in there. It is!

Years ago I ran across a quote from an author named Timothy Gallwey:

> When we plant a rose seed in the earth, we notice that it is small, but we do not criticize it as "rootless and stemless." We treat it as a seed, giving it the water and nourishment required of a seed. When it first shoots up out of the earth, we don't condemn it as immature and under-developed; nor do we criticize the buds for not being open when they appear. We stand in wonder at the process taking place and give the plant the care it needs at each stage of its development. The rose is a rose from the time it is a seed

> to the time it dies. Within it, at all times, it contains its whole potential. . . . At each stage, at each moment, it is perfectly all right as it is (*The Inner Game of Tennis* [New York: Bantam Books, 1987], 29).

Can you see how that applies to us as children of God? Sometimes, instead of standing in wonder at the process of our becoming good and better, we criticize ourselves. I wish we could do that less and rejoice in our progress more.

I know this whole growing process takes a lot of time, patience, diligence, and experience. A seed doesn't pop out of the ground with corn ready for a picnic or pumpkins ready to carve in a couple of days.

What if you had a little bag with a bunch of seeds all mixed together—dozens and hundreds of "no-names"? Would you want to plant some, having no idea what you would get? Spooky!

That is why we go to the Carpenter's Seed store and look for packages that have the right seeds, just as we go to Carpenter Seed and look for what we want to plant. In fact, if you happen to be in the Provo area, you might drop by Carpenter Seed and ask where the charity seed package is. Maybe someone in the store will have read this little chapter, and they'll smile and direct you to the carrots.

HIGHLY RECOMMENDED READING

Seed packages.
Alma 32.

CHAPTER 10

Filtering and Purifying Our Thoughts

When I lived in Africa, I had to both filter and purify the water I drank. This is no small thing. There was no other way to get a drink of water than the long way, the hard way—if living and feeling well were important. And they were.

Filtering takes out a lot of the impurities that may be visible to the naked eye, but without purifying, there are still things in the water that can make you sick. If you skip either step, there are usually unpleasant consequences, some immediate, some more long-lasting.

In a similar way, that which we take into our minds, our hearts, and our souls must be filtered and purified. The consequences of impurities are so much greater when we speak of our thoughts than when we speak of water or food.

In a world where it sometimes seems that nothing is sacred

anymore, where "anything goes," and where there are almost no boundaries or fences, it is more difficult AND more important to purify our thoughts.

One of the most common scriptural references used in connection with our thoughts is Doctrine and Covenants 121:45: "Let virtue garnish thy thoughts unceasingly." Why speak of purifying our thoughts, and of letting virtue garnish our thoughts unceasingly, to good people? Is this a challenge? Even with Latter-day Saints? Even with people who attend sacrament meeting, hold family home evening, read scriptures, follow the Golden Rule, and watch BYU-TV?

Even.

Our character is shaped by what our minds are focused on—what our hearts truly desire. Consider this poem from the book *As a Man Thinketh* by James Allen:

> *Mind is the Master-power that moulds and makes,*
> *And Man is Mind, and evermore he takes*
> *The tool of Thought, and, shaping what he wills,*
> *Brings forth a thousand joys, a thousand ills:—*
> *He thinks in secret, and it comes to pass:*
> *Environment is but his looking-glass.*

We simply cannot become what we're NOT thinking about. And we cannot avoid becoming what we ARE thinking about. As the oft-quoted passage from Proverbs 23:7 says: "For as [a man] thinketh in his heart, so is he."

A visiting teaching message from several years ago offered this reminder: "We don't develop character by chance. Good character is the result of continual effort in righteous thinking and the righteous acts that such thinking brings about. . . . Clearly, we are what we think. And if we think righteous thoughts, we will very likely live righteously" ("Charity Thinketh No Evil," *Ensign*, August 1988, 61).

In Alma 37:36, Alma gives counsel to his son Helaman: "Cry unto God for all thy support; yea, let all thy doings be unto the Lord, and whithersoever thou goest let it be in the Lord; yea, *let all thy thoughts be directed unto the Lord;* yea, let the affections of thy heart be placed upon the Lord forever" (emphasis added).

We DO become what we think about, what we allow to come into our minds and STAY. And we really do eventually receive the true desires of our hearts. Think how wonderful it will be if our affections are "placed upon the Lord forever"!

I like the story of a woman who was asked to give a talk about sacrifice in sacrament meeting. She said that in preparing her remarks she had wanted to experience sacrifice, and had given it a lot of thought.

For many years (I think she said twenty-five), she had watched a certain soap opera on TV. She apparently had tried to stop a few times but hadn't been successful. She knew she would miss the characters, who had become like real people to her. She even said that some of her children told her, "Mom, you don't seem like the kind of person who would be hooked on a 'soap'!"

The more she thought about it, the more she realized that this was the sacrifice she needed to make as she prepared to speak in sacrament meeting. She said she did it "cold turkey," and she was successful in breaking her addiction.

Then she spoke of the blessings that had come to her. She said, "It's not just the extra five hours I have each week . . . it's the feeling that I'm FREE!" She felt like she had been trapped in some awful artificial world, she said. One part of her freedom was that she could use her mind to think of much more uplifting things than whether Bernella had really poisoned Bernard (or whatever).

One of the cunning and effective tools of the enemy of our souls is to get us to dwell on evil and idle thoughts. As Elder Spencer J. Condie has said:

> Satan would have us waste our time in activities that impede our progress on the pathway to perfection. [Addiction is an enemy to agency.] Many people lead empty lives completely devoid of purpose, meaning, and direction. Empty lives must be filled with something, anything, so some people fill their empty lives with endless hours of television, while others become addicted to pornography, alcohol, tobacco, and other drugs. . . . And ever so surely these individuals trade their moral agency for their addiction until they are no longer able to exercise their agency. All of their decisions are now on automatic pilot, with seemingly little hope of changing the direction of their lives. There is little advantage to living in a free country if we are in bondage to personal habits ("Agency: The Gift of Choices," *Ensign*, September 1995, 20).

President Gordon B. Hinckley has often warned us about the particular bondage of pornographic material, which can capture our thoughts so easily. He said:

> There is so much of filth and lust and pornography in this world. We as Latter-day Saints must rise above it and stand tall against it. You can't afford to indulge in it. You just cannot afford to indulge in it. You have to keep it out of your heart. Like tobacco it's addictive, and it will destroy those who tamper with it. "Let virtue garnish thy thoughts unceasingly."
>
> Of course you are tempted. It seems as if the whole world has become obsessed with sex. In a very beguiling and alluring way, it is thrown at you constantly. You are exposed to it on television, in magazines and books, in videos, even in music. Turn your back on it. Shun it. I know that is easy to say, and difficult to do. But each time that you do so, it will be so much the easier the next time. What a wonderful thing it will be if someday you can stand before the Lord and say, "I am clean" ("Be Ye Clean," *Ensign*, May 1996, 48).

We MUST let virtue garnish our thoughts unceasingly. Otherwise our thoughts can lead to evil deeds and even to addictions. Some become addicted to pornography, some to gambling (such as lotteries and poker), or to shallow reading, time-wasting games, gossip, spending beyond their means, overeating, work, leisure, sports, or any number of things. And too often, one addiction leads to another.

Any and all such addictions may interfere with our ability to exercise agency and enjoy the blessing of pure thoughts!

King Benjamin taught this powerful lesson about our thoughts:

> And finally, I cannot tell you all the things whereby ye may commit sin; for there are divers ways and means, even so many that I cannot number them.
>
> But this much I can tell you, that if ye do not watch yourselves, and your thoughts, and your words, and your deeds, and observe the commandments of God, and continue in the faith of what ye have heard concerning the coming of our Lord, even unto the end of your lives, ye must perish. And now, O man, remember, and perish not (Mosiah 4:29–30).

Thoughts are so POWERFUL! They can lead us up or down, or they can park us on some plateau. They can help us become more Christlike and Godlike, or they can put us in bondage to bad habits and addictions.

If we're thinking a thought that is not good, it's much easier to pluck it out of our minds when it first starts, just as it's easiest to pluck out weeds when they're tiny. It becomes so HARD to get thoughts and weeds out if we let them stick around and get roots. This is especially true for the thoughts we feed, nourish, focus on, and entertain.

I remember a little story of a teacher who asked the children in her class to think about a big hippopotamus in a river. She described the hippo in a lot of detail. He was bright blue, with large, white polka dots all over his body. She had the children imagine the bright blue hippo with the white dots rolling around in the river and the mud. She kept emphasizing each detail.

Then, all of a sudden, the teacher said, "Stop!" She asked the students NOT to think about the blue hippo anymore. But by then it was too late. The image was planted solidly in their minds, and it was very difficult for them to think of anything else.

The teacher then taught them the importance of paying attention to what they were thinking and not just letting their minds "drift." How does that little saying go? "The idle mind is the devil's workshop."

Do you have a big blue hippo that sometimes wallows into your thoughts? Have you figured out some strategies for ignoring him, or for consciously putting a more powerful image in his place?

Can you think of a time when you've been able to change your thoughts and thus change your response or reaction to some event or circumstance? If you haven't written down what happened, I encourage you to do so. We can allow our own experiences to be our teachers. Whatever worked for you then could work for you again.

As I've pondered the idea of filtering and purifying our thoughts, I've thought that filtering might be the equivalent of not letting certain thoughts into our minds in the first place.

Picture our eyes and ears on one side of the filter, and our minds on the other side. The filter would stop inappropriate things from coming through our ears or our eyes into our minds.

Then we do the purifying between our minds and our hearts. Sometimes our minds might be quite taken with something we inadvertently see or hear, but our hearts will sense the danger and give us a warning.

Any thought—either good or bad—starts out small and is easy to pluck out of our minds when it first gets in there. If the teacher in our story, for example, had just told the students to think about a hippo but had changed the subject and helped them put something else in their minds, they wouldn't have had such a hard time stopping the image from coming back.

Our challenge is to pluck out the bad thoughts, and to protect and nurture the good thoughts. Starve and pluck out the bad ones, feed and nurture the good ones. Decide what we will keep and what we can't afford to keep.

In both the New Testament and the Book of Mormon, we are taught that charity includes thinking no evil (see 1 Corinthians 13:4–5 and Moroni 7:45). But what if things just accidentally pop into our minds? We have to figure out a way to cast them out.

One thing I like to do is to memorize scriptures, hymns, good songs, and thoughts that I particularly like. We can't replace the blue hippo with anything if we don't have anything at the ready.

I invite you to read the preface in the hymn book. There are some incredible reminders of why we should use the hymns more often in our personal study, our talks and lessons, and just to help with keeping our thoughts clean and pure.

I write things I want to memorize on three-by-five cards and put them in a little two-hole notebook that I keep in my car. It's amazing how much I can memorize as I keep things close like that.

I remember when missionaries were memorizing Doctrine and Covenants 4, one of the ways they did it was to put the first letter for the words that came in a list, such as "hmms" for heart, might, mind, and strength. Or "fhcl" for faith, hope, charity and love. Or "f, v, k, t, p, bk, g, c, h, d" for "remember faith, virtue, knowledge, temperance, patience, brotherly kindness, godliness, charity, humility, diligence" (D&C 4:6).

Some have suggested that to memorize scriptures it helps to put the first letters of each word in the verse on an index card or a Post-It note and have those handy to jog your memory.

Sometimes all you need is a key letter or a key word. Key words help me when I'm memorizing hymns. I can remember when I first memorized "I Stand All Amazed" (*Hymns,* no. 193); I'd remember the words "I stand," "I marvel," and "I think," and away I'd go.

Years ago I learned a little thought that helped me in memorizing, but now I can't remember it exactly. Quit laughing. It went something like this: Read it out loud once an hour for a day. (I don't think it meant for twenty-four hours—just for when you're awake.) Read it out loud once a day for a week. Read it out loud once a week for a month. Read it out loud once a month for a year. Then it's yours.

Again, I emphasize that it's not enough just to try to stop thinking of the hippo—he has to be REPLACED with something that you DO want to think about.

It's not easy to change your mind—to change your thoughts (and thus to have control over your actions, your behavior), but it's possible, and it's critical.

What was the counsel President Hinckley's father gave to him when he (President Hinckley) was so discouraged while serving his mission in England? "Forget yourself and go to work!" He was asking him to change his thoughts.

Another great strategy is to ask yourself the wonderful question, "What would Jesus do?" Perhaps this has been suggested so many times for so many things that it has lost some of its effectiveness for you. But think about it—have you had an experience where you actually asked that question in your heart, or something like it: "What would Jesus want me to do right now?" Has it helped? It's made a dramatic difference for me on many occasions.

Choose good things to read, including the scriptures, the hymn book, the *Ensign,* the *New Era,* the *Friend,* the weekly *Church News,* and good books. Ask others whose opinions you value to suggest good books and articles. Share with others, and they'll likely share with you as well.

The things we read become the things we think about. They're all stored in our minds somewhere. Sometimes we watch TV, go to a movie, read a book or magazine or whatever with NO THOUGHT (literally) about what words or ideas or seeds may be planted in our minds and hearts as a result. How much nicer it will be if we have a whole supply of good food for thought! Maybe this is like food storage for the brain, mind, and heart. You have to give your mind good things to think about!

Perspective is helpful, isn't it? I love the phrase from "Let the Holy Spirit Guide" (*Hymns,* no. 143) when we sing "He [the Holy Ghost] will testify of Christ, Light our minds with heaven's view." Keeping our minds and hearts focused on why we are here and who we are can help us to stay positive and pressing forward. If we get stuck in the here and now and lose our perspective, it is easy to be overcome with negative thoughts, dead-end worries, and unfounded fear.

The temple is a place for thinking good thoughts. When I'm there I feel like my ability to think is enhanced. Somehow I'm able to think more clearly, to get rid of some of the "static." Even going near a temple and spending time on the grounds (which are always beautiful) is edifying and soothing.

Going for walks is an ideal time to think. Even "power walkers" are thinking as they speed along. I'm more the sauntering type, and when I'm out early in the morning, I'm especially aware of the beauty around me and I have some wonderful conversations with my Heavenly Father. And if I'm walking with someone else, I have wonderful conversations with them.

Music can make such a difference. I have been especially moved by certain types of music, and I make it a point to stick with the kind that lifts my spirits and inspires me. From Mozart to McLean, Handel to Hilary, Grobin to Gladys, from the Tabernacle Choir to Peter Shickele (PDQ Bach!), from Dyer to Il Divo . . . I love music!

Pray earnestly for Heavenly help. I think we probably have

only a tiny little awareness of how much help is available if we'll just ask and seek and knock! There is an abundance of specific, powerful help—we just need to "tap in" to the Source!

Now, here's an idea I especially want you to pay attention to and not skip over. CHOOSE things to think about. Yes. Something interesting—like stars, or ants, or bridges, or baby fat—or faith, or charity, or the Atonement—or Helen Keller, or Michelangelo, or Gandhi, or Socrates, or ancient Egypt—or any topic that might take you to some wonderful studying and learning.

I've mentioned gratitude in another chapter, but I want to say that counting your many blessings and naming them one by one can give you many happy surprises and the blessing of thinking good thoughts.

There are so many other strategies, including the unfailing blessings of prayer, scripture study, temple attendance, service, fasting . . . the basics!

You likely have other strategies, and I hope you'll share your ideas with others and get some of theirs.

Elder Stephen D. Nadauld suggested that we do an inventory of our thoughts:

> As people individually or collectively experience conditions that may lead unwittingly to their own downfall, what can be done? I would like to recommend three steps that can help. First, Jacob acknowledged that the people had begun to have inappropriate thoughts: thoughts of gain, of advantage, of status, of power, of lust. How useful it would be from time to time to take an inventory of our thoughts and the

> feelings of our hearts. Such an examination might involve asking questions like, What do I spend time thinking about? Do I ever feel uneasy about my thoughts? How do my thoughts compare with concepts taught in the scriptures and by spiritual leaders? Have I read the Sermon on the Mount lately, and do I understand its applications? Am I nervous, anxious, and upset, or calm and confident? ("Pride: A Challenge from Within," *Ensign*, July 1996, 19).

Becoming increasingly aware of our thoughts can help us to recognize the need to keep working at the filtering and purifying.

We need to do more pondering and meditating. Has it been a while since you've just sat and *thought*? President Boyd K. Packer said that "thoughts are talks we hold with ourselves" ("The Spirit of Revelation," *Ensign*, November 1999, 24). I don't think I do enough of this—of talking to myself, of pondering, of really thinking carefully and considering deeply.

Hopefully you've read some ideas you can use to help you filter and purify your thoughts. One more great key to help us choose wisely is found in Moroni 7:12–13: "Wherefore, all things which are good cometh of God; and that which is evil cometh of the devil; for the devil is an enemy unto God, and fighteth against him continually, and inviteth and enticeth to sin, and to do that which is evil continually. But behold, that which is of God inviteth and enticeth to do good continually; wherefore, every thing which inviteth and enticeth to do good, and to love God, and to serve him, is inspired of God."

And I'll add the thirteenth Article of Faith: "We believe in being honest, true, chaste, benevolent, virtuous, and in doing good to all men; indeed, we may say that we follow the admonition of Paul—We believe all things, we hope all things, we have endured many things, and hope to be able to endure all things. If there is anything virtuous, lovely, or of good report or praiseworthy, we seek after these things."

Yes! That is a good pattern to follow.

May our conscious efforts to filter and purify our thoughts lead us to the wonderful blessings of hope, joy, and peace of conscience and soul.

I am convinced that as we control our thoughts, we also can conquer and discipline and guide our actions, our words, and our lives. And then when Jesus asks, "What's on your mind?" we'll not hesitate to have Him know our thoughts, immediately, openly, and honestly. Let's get ready for His question!

HIGHLY RECOMMENDED READING

James Allen, *As a Man Thinketh,* Mount Vernon, NY: The Peter Pauper Press.

"The Visiting Teacher: Charity Thinketh No Evil," *Ensign,* August 1988, 61.

Anne Osborn Poelman, *The Amulek Alternative: Exercising Agency in a World of Choice,* Salt Lake City: Deseret Book, 1997.

Norman Vincent Peale, *The Power of Positive Thinking,* New Jersey: Prentice-Hall, Inc., 1956.

CHAPTER 11

The Real World

You've probably noticed, as I have, all the ads for reality TV. These are programs that show real people doing real things, right? Sure—on a remote island somewhere in the Pacific.

There are people who allow coverage of their daily lives, or contests where we get to follow an amazing race. There are shows where people swap mothers or fight "on camera." There are shows where people try to become an apprentice, an American idol, a survivor, a model, a weight-loss champion, or just plain popular.

But is it real? Maybe, maybe not.

Joseph Walker, a television critic, shares these insights about the media world:

> One reason TV and the movies distort life is that

> many of those who make the films and sitcoms are out of touch with the fulness of the truth.
>
> There are a few things I learned very early in my career as a television critic:
>
> • No problem is so big that it can't be solved in twenty-three minutes (thirty, counting commercials);
>
> • For all of its talk about public service and art, commercial television exists to sell soap;
>
> • There is often no discernible correlation between the real world and Hollywood's perception of reality.
>
> If you watch much television, you already know about the first two items—especially if you've heard about the TV ratings system and how it works.
>
> But you may not be as familiar with Hollywood's skewed view of the world in which we live—a view that, more often than not, finds itself at odds with eternal truth ("Reel Life vs. Real Life," *Ensign*, June 1993, 15–16).

I recommend his whole article, which reveals some of the REAL truths about Hollywood.

One day I got in the mail an envelope with bold letters on the front asking this question: "Where do you go for the truth?" Then there was a message just underneath: "Please open immediately." They wanted me to subscribe to a magazine, and it wasn't the *Ensign*.

I'm so happy to know sources of truth, sources of light, sources that help me sort the real from the false.

I saved a page from a magazine years ago that showed a

cowboy on a horse in some beautiful mountain country. He was leading another horse, which had a body bag draped over it. The ad had this message at the top: "What if cigarette ads told the truth?" It actually looked like an ad for cigarettes! In the box that usually has a warning from the Surgeon General, it says: "YEE HAW! You Too Can Be an Independent, Rugged, Macho-looking Dead Guy."

Much about the world we live in is fuzzy. It's as if anyone can put a "spin" on information and make it the opposite of what it was meant to be. I see so many things for sale that are promoted as "looking like the real thing." We used to use the word *fake,* but now I think it's PC to use *faux* (pronounced "foe," if I'm not wrong). You can acquire faux pearls, fur, diamonds, leather, whipped cream, wood, purses, and even faux relationships.

Think of the times when you've heard a phrase like "Welcome to the REAL world!" When someone says that, they're usually trying to get you to face what THEY feel is "reality," to get your head out of the clouds, back on your neck. "Hey, Mildred! You've been living in a bubble! A time warp! Come on out of there and join us in the REAL world!"

Even in articles and discussions we sometimes speak of preparing young people to "live in the real world." We generally describe the skills they need in order to live successfully.

Sometimes those returning from missions or other life-changing experiences hear phrases like "welcome back to the real world," with talk of adjusting, fitting back in, returning to being and doing as they were before they left. What's peculiar about that?

I used to hear missionaries at the Missionary Training Center talk about what it would be like when they got back to the "real world." I wanted to say to them (and often did), "THIS is the real world! Right here, right now." Here they were, striving to become effective servants of the Lord, to bring people out of the darkness into His marvelous light, where they could see things as they really are, and as they really will be (see Jacob 4:13). What could be more real than that?

All around us we have evidence of things we cannot see, but that are real (see Hebrews 1:1). Perhaps it's been true forever that the things that are uncommon, peculiar, holy, and set apart are the things that are REAL. The places, the experiences, the motivation, the future, the travelers we meet along the way. The real world is along the upward line, and there is really no substitute for what is real.

Once upon a time, a big family went to a restaurant for lunch. Tables were put together, and the waitress began to take orders from the various family members.

She came to a little fellow about six years old and asked, "What would you like?" It was an awkward moment as he looked toward his mother to order for him. She wasn't sure what to do, since the waitress was continuing to look at the little boy rather than the mother.

So the little fellow got pretty excited and said, "I'd like a hot dog!" That instantly caused the mother to say something like,

"Oh, no, he'll have . . ." and she chose something different. Probably asparagus casserole or faux meatloaf.

The waitress, still focused on the little boy, asked, "And what would you like on your hot dog?"

Oh, my goodness! What would happen now? Suddenly everything was very, very awkward and quiet. The mother, caught off guard, remained silent.

The little boy said he would like ketchup, mustard, and relish, and the waitress wrote it all down, finished taking the other people's orders, and left.

The boy, amazed, turned to his mother and said, "She thinks I'm real!"

In this world there are so many people who are treated as if they don't exist—as if THEY'RE not real, and they don't matter. Ouch.

When Lehi dreamed, he saw a great and spacious building (see 1 Nephi 8:26–27, 31–34). It was "filled with people, both old and young, both male and female; and their manner of dress was exceedingly fine; and they were in the attitude of mocking and pointing their fingers towards those who had come at and were partaking of the fruit" (v. 27).

Lehi saw other multitudes feeling their way toward the GAS building (Great and Spacious . . . my friends know how much I like acronyms). He saw that once they entered they began pointing the finger of scorn at Lehi and all who were partaking of the fruit. It seems there have always been those who have become anti-light and anti-truth, and whose hearts have been stirred up to anger against that which is good (see 2 Nephi 28:20). And they do their best to make people who are trying to behave differently feel "not real."

When I read about those in the great and spacious building pointing fingers and mocking, I remember what the Lord said to Moroni: "fools mock, but they shall mourn" (Ether 12:26). I guess those in the GAS building don't realize how foolish they really look and really are. They act at times as if they think THEY'RE the ones in charge.

Maybe you have had the opportunity (I smile a little to use that particular word) to receive the scorn and finger-pointing from some who, in their exceedingly fine-twined linens, seem not to be able to leave you alone. I like the way Elder L. Aldin Porter wrote about this:

> The wicked heap scorn when they have no other weapons to use, and too often the righteous run for cover, especially if the mocker can run fast or jump high or sing well or has high-profile degrees or a great deal of money, even if each or all have nothing to do with the subject at hand.
>
> I ask you, what are the rewards of standing fast in your own virtue, even against the scorn of the world? They are far more monumental than one might think ("But We Heeded Them Not," *Ensign*, August 1998, 7).

That is thought-provoking for me—to consider the blessings (rewards) waiting for those who are true and faithful.

Isn't it true that we often listen to voices of those who have NO CLUE what is real, who live in an artificial world where they think they can buy anything with money? The wonderful thing Lehi says is: "but we heeded them not." Wow. He knew what was real and what wasn't, and he knew the danger of even responding to the scorn.

The powerful lesson continues in verse 34: "For as many as heeded them, had fallen away." Don't pay attention! They'll pull you down and away! It is a matter of life and death (really) that we stick with what is real, holding on to an iron rod and following a path that is strait and narrow.

But oh, isn't it sometimes hard not to hear the noise and see the sights of the world—of the GAS building? Elder Glenn L. Pace reminded us that the inhabitants of that building are not really happy:

> Even though you have a testimony and want to do what is right, it is difficult not to be drawn to the great and spacious building. From all appearances, the people in the building seem to be having a great time. The music and laughter are deafening. You would say to me what my children have said, "They're not really happy, huh, Dad?" as you watch them party.
>
> They look happy and free, but don't mistake telestial pleasure for celestial happiness and joy. Don't mistake lack of self-control for freedom. Complete freedom without appropriate restraint makes us slaves to our appetites. Don't envy a lesser and lower life. . . .
>
> To those of you who are inching your way closer and closer to that great and spacious building, let me make it completely clear that the people in that

> building have absolutely nothing to offer except instant, short-term gratification inescapably connected to long-term sorrow and suffering. The commandments you observe were not given by a dispassionate God to prevent you from having fun, but by a loving Father in Heaven who wants you to be happy while you are living on this earth as well as in the hereafter ("They're Not Really Happy," *Ensign*, November 1987, 40).

Think of the truth that he has shared: The only thing offered in the GAS building and by those who are part of it is "instant, short-term gratification inescapably connected to long-term sorrow and suffering." It's like the advice we've all heard many times: "Don't trade what you want MOST for what you want now." Indeed!

That brings us back to the statement from Alma's teaching to his son Corianton: "Wickedness never was happiness" (Alma 41:10). And it never EVER will be, no matter how popular or prevalent it becomes, and no matter how many are supportive of it and immersed in it.

Whatever they seem to have in the GAS building is faux. Faux, faux, faux! Fee fi faux fum! Even GIANTS know it isn't real!

There is so much that's fake about life in and near the GAS building. From artificial light to artificial joy, from artificial laughter to artificial relationships, there is really nothing of eternal worth in or anywhere near this worldly, unreal place that has no foundation.

The Savior said, "No man can serve two masters: for either he will hate the one, and love the other; or else he will hold to the one, and despise the other. Ye cannot serve God and mammon" (Matthew 6:24). We can't straddle the line between the two, can we? I really like the way Elder Marion G. Romney said it at a BYU devotional in 1955: "Now there are those among us who are trying to serve the Lord without offending the devil" (as quoted by James E. Faust, "Serving the Lord and Resisting the Devil," *Ensign*, September 1995, 2).

Isn't that a great way to express it! It's impossible to strive to be better without "offending the devil"! So we DO have to choose. Do we want to love and serve the Lord (and thus offend the devil)? Whom shall we choose to follow, and whom shall we choose to hate? Can you even put those words in your head!—that you would choose to serve and follow the devil and hate the Lord? It hurts even to THINK of it!

We're told not to touch unclean things and not to succumb to worldliness. We're to keep ourselves unspotted from the things of the world. That's one of the tricky things about being IN the world but not OF the world. "Be not conformed to this world" (Romans 12:2).

So we strive to reach a point where the world and worldliness can't touch us. We can be an influence, but we cannot be influenced, no matter how much fun the GAS crowd seems to be having (*seems* being an important word in the thought).

I keep getting this feeling about the GAS crowd that there are those, however few, who know they're in the wrong place heading the wrong direction, and are searching for a way out.

They've chosen misery when what they really wanted was joy, and they feel trapped. They're searching for the real world. Maybe our light can help them choose another way.

There are things we can do to improve this world we live in while at the same time looking forward to a better one. We even sing, "Have I done any good in the world today?" The next part of the question is "Have I helped anyone in need?" (*Hymns*, no. 223). OUR reality is not mocking but helping, not pointing a finger of scorn, but offering a kind hand.

I've always learned a lot from reading what Brother Hugh Nibley has written. He had the ability to pull away the cobwebs and help me see things as they really are. Here is an example:

> Nothing is more real in this life than the constant awareness that things could be better than they are. The Atonement does not take full effect in this world at all, and hereafter it will take effect completely only when this world is made part of the celestial order. The unreality is all on this side of the great and awful gulf. If there is anything manifestly evident about the doings in the great and spacious building (see 1 Ne. 11:36), it is the hollow laughter and silly pretensions of the people in it. Today the sense of unreality is beginning to haunt us all—life has become a TV spectacular to which we are beginning to adapt our own behavior. In this age of theatromania, where everything is a contrived spectacle, our lives reflect an endless procession of futility. . . . The rigorous terms of the Atonement, which demands the active

> participation of all its beneficiaries and passes the bitter cup of sacrifice to all of them, has made it unpopular to the point of total rejection by the general public—hardly a product of wishful thinking or human invention! ("The Atonement of Jesus Christ, Part 4," *Ensign*, October 1990, 28).

There is so much in what he has shared that catches my attention and makes me want to think more about it, and talk about it.

Whom shall we follow? After whom shall we pattern our lives—our homes, our families, our choices, our direction? Whom shall we love and serve?

I have felt for most of my life that one reason we're asked to become as a little child is so that we can strive to be REAL. Isn't it refreshing to meet someone and feel that "what you see is what you get"? True blue, through and through.

One of the nicest compliments I ever received came to me one day when a returned sister missionary visited me at the MTC. I asked about her mission and we caught up a bit, and then she asked, "Do you know why all of us love you so much?" My answer was, "Because you know how much I love you?" She said, "It's because you never wore a mask." Maybe that won't strike you as being much of a compliment, but it meant and still means so MUCH to me because I have tried to be who I really am, to be genuine, to figure out the best I can what it means to be as a child.

If you're interested in the concept of "real," I think you'd enjoy reading again *The Velveteen Rabbit.* It's a delightful little book.

This is the story of a splendid velveteen rabbit that was in a boy's stocking on Christmas morning. The story tells of the rabbit's relationship with the other toys, many of which were more expensive and seemingly superior. The rabbit felt insignificant.

There is an interchange one day between the rabbit and the wise old skin horse:

> "What is REAL?" asked the Rabbit one day, when they were lying side by side near the nursery fender, before Nana came to tidy the room. "Does it mean having things that buzz inside you and a stick-out handle?"
>
> "Real isn't how you are made," said the Skin Horse. "It's a thing that happens to you. When a child loves you for a long, long time, not just to play with, but REALLY loves you, then you become Real."
>
> "Does it hurt?" asked the Rabbit.
>
> "Sometimes," said the Skin Horse, for he was always truthful. "When you are Real you don't mind being hurt."
>
> "Does it happen all at once, like being wound up," he asked, "or bit by bit?"
>
> "It doesn't happen all at once," said the Skin Horse. "You become. It takes a long time. That's why it doesn't happen often to people who break easily, or have sharp edges, or who have to be carefully kept. Generally, by the time you are Real, most of your hair

> has been loved off, and your eyes drop out and you get loose in the joints and very shabby. But these things don't matter at all, because once you are Real you can't be ugly, except to people who don't understand."
>
> "I suppose you are real?" said the Rabbit. And then he wished he had not said it, for he thought the Skin Horse might be sensitive. But the Skin Horse only smiled.
>
> "The Boy's Uncle made me Real," he said. "That was a great many years ago; but once you are Real you can't become unreal again. It lasts for always" (Margery Williams, *The Velveteen Rabbit,* or *How Toys Become Real* [Garden City, NY: Doubleday, 1975], 16–20).

As my parents grew older, even as they lost their hair and their joints got looser and all, they were real. Not ugly, but REAL.

For just a moment, will you think with me about the possibility that the REAL world is the one we look forward to? And that our efforts to make a difference in this world in which we now live are efforts toward making it REAL?

All that is real and true calls to us to be better, to reach higher, to come unto Christ and follow Him.

Let us have eyes to see things as they really are, and ears to hear things that are really true, and hearts that follow the straight and narrow path, and hands that hold tight to the iron rod.

Truth and light are real.

Knowing we are children of God is real.

Knowing that He loves us dearly and constantly is real.

He really DID send His Holy Son to be the Savior and Redeemer of the world.

The plan of happiness is real.

There really ARE consequences for our choices, for the exercise of our God-given agency.

Christ really WILL come again.

We really WILL be judged for our thoughts, the desires of our heart, and our actions.

There really IS a Heaven, and there really IS a way to be there forever.

We really ARE brothers and sisters, and we really DO have responsibility to exercise charity toward each other.

That, in part, is what I mean by the real world.

As Emma Smith was told in Doctrine and Covenants 25:10, "And verily I say unto thee that thou shalt lay aside the things of this world, and seek for the things of a better."

Let's be GOOD, and let's be TRUE.

Let's stand closer together and be kinder and more supportive of each other.

May we do our best to share the GOOD NEWS with others.

They NEED this message! They need it NOW!

They NEED the peace, the happiness, the contentment, gratitude, safety, and the JOY that are part of the gospel of Jesus Christ.

Jesus Christ announced Himself as the light and life of the

world, and following Him the best we can will allow us to see and experience things as they really are, not as someone tries to make them appear.

God sees and comprehends things as they really are, and oh what a difference it will make in our decisions, our choices, our direction, and our eventual destination if we "tune in" to the ways in which He is trying to influence us to choose the right.

Oh, and by the way, "welcome to the REAL WORLD!"

HIGHLY RECOMMENDED READING

Glenn L. Pace, "They're Not Really Happy," *Ensign*, November 1987, 39–41.

Joseph Walker, "Reel Life vs. Real Life," *Ensign*, June 1993, 15–19.

Sheryl Condie Kempton, " 'But That's My Show!': Weighing the Value of Watching Television," *Ensign*, August 1986, 54–56.

Neil and Joan Flinders, "A Home Is Also a House," *Ensign*, November 1973, 20–25.

Quinn G. McKay, "All That Glitters Isn't Celestial," *Ensign*, June 1987, 20–22.

CHAPTER 12

Follow the Prophet

Have you ever been standing in line to check out at the store, leaning on your basket, and noticed the headlines on the tabloids stacked at eye level right in your path?

Aren't some of them wild and wacko? Have you ever found yourself thinking, "Who buys these things!?"

Well . . . I did. I couldn't resist. When I saw the headline and the picture, I said to myself, "Self, you MUST have this!"

I don't know where it is anymore, but I still have the cover. The headline was: "Noah's Ark Discovered!" Yes! And there was a picture of the Ark! I'm not kidding!

And OH, I wish I could find the whole paper, because it obviously had answers to some exceedingly important questions and mysteries. I apologize for having let it sink into the matter unorganized in my basement. It had such promising subheads:

"God's Warning of a Second Great Flood." (Well, not even the best newspapers get it right every single time, eh?)

"Secrets of Daily Life in Heaven." (They've been reading the Doctrine and Covenants again.)

So I brought the tabloid home and thought and thought about it. It was called *The Sun*. I began thinking of the Son who created the sun—as in sunshine and light of the day and all that (NOT the tabloid).

And then I got a feeling of DUH (I'm smiling). I've known "forever" that we don't need a tabloid to remind us of what we need to be doing! We have the Son Himself, and he communicates through a living prophet. No extra charge!

Elder John H. Groberg once told of an experience he had in Tonga when he was a missionary. He was prompted to visit a missionary who was ill who lived on a somewhat distant island. He went to the missionary, administered to him, and then received a strong impression to get him back to the main island. It was stormy, and there was anxiety among the eight passengers on the boat.

There was a dangerous reef near the small opening through which they had to pass as they got closer to their destination. Unless they hit the opening exactly, they'd be smashed against the reef. They all looked for the small light that marked the opening.

At the moment when many were feeling panic, Elder Groberg said he looked at the captain and saw a calmness as his eyes penetrated the darkness ahead. Quietly he said "Ko e Maama e" ("There is the light.") Elder Groberg pointed out that although HE could not see the light, the captain could. He was not fooled by the storm, nor was he influenced by the pleadings of those who had much less experience and may have wanted him to turn to the left or the right ("There Is the Light," *Ensign*, November 1976, 44–45).

Elder Groberg taught a powerful lesson: There IS a living prophet whose eyes can see further and better than ours, and who can help us find the light and guide us safely home. His is the voice that speaks clearly no matter how terrible the storms may be or how dark the night may get. I can depend on his experience and knowledge to keep me in the right way as I learn and follow.

I suppose it IS peculiar to believe in continuing revelation from God to His children through a prophet—that there is a man living who can, with authority, teach us what God wants us to know and do and be.

In the early days of missionary work in the Philippines, a group of us missionaries spent a "D Day" (now "P Day") visiting some caves at a place called Montalbon. These were not the sort of caves where there are guides and specified places to walk, with lights along the walls. We hiked deep into a cave, even walking in some water. At some point we stopped and began to share our feelings with each other. We talked of our desire to help things move from our one branch and about 100 members (in the entire Philippine Islands!) to many more who would accept the gospel and come unto Christ.

We decided to turn off our flashlights and blow out our candles. Oh, it was so dark! You could put your hand right in front of your face and not see anything at all! So we talked of the responsibility and joy of helping people come from darkness to light.

Someone suggested we sing a hymn there in the darkness, and the one we all knew was "We Thank Thee, O God, for a Prophet" (*Hymns,* no. 19). How interesting the words were in that particular setting! " . . . to lighten our minds with its rays." "There is hope smiling brightly before us." " . . . bask in its life-giving light."

And the hymn ends with another truth: "they who reject this glad message shall never such happiness know." Ouch!

I've loved that hymn in a different way since my experience in a deep, dark cave in 1964.

When we finished singing, we lit one match. One little match. And oh! The darkness dispelled by that little light! I almost wanted to sing a little song I learned in 4-H about "this little 4-H light of mine, I'm going to let it shine!" But this was for us a symbol of the light of the gospel, and Christ as the Light of the World, showing the way Home to any who would notice and follow.

We did indeed thank God for a prophet!

(And by the way, there are more than half a million members in the Philippines now, fourteen missions, and a temple.)

In April 1992, President Gordon B. Hinckley gave a talk to the youth and young adults of the Church. He quoted 1 Peter 2:9: "Ye are a chosen generation, a royal priesthood, an holy nation, a peculiar people; that ye should shew forth the praises of him who hath called you out of darkness into his marvellous light," and then said:

> I know of no other statement which more aptly describes you, nor which sets before you a higher ideal by which to shape and guide your lives. . . .
>
> With worthiness in your lives, you may enjoy the comforting, protecting, guiding influence of ministering angels. No individual of earthly royalty has a blessing as great. Live for it. Be worthy of it, is my plea to each of you.
>
> Peter speaks of "an holy nation." He does not refer to a political entity. He refers to a vast congregation of the Saints of God, men and women who walk in holiness before Him and who look to Jesus Christ as their Savior and their King. . . .
>
> And so I invite you, every one of you within the sound of my voice, to think for a moment upon why you are here under the divine plan of your Father in Heaven and of your tremendous potential to do good during the life that He has given you.
>
> Please know that we love you. We appreciate you. We have confidence in you, knowing that it will only be a short time until you must take over the leadership of this church and of other great responsibilities which may be yours in the world in which you will live ("A Chosen Generation," *Ensign,* May 1992, 71).

This is obviously a talk I would encourage you to read again (no matter how old or young you are). But I'm thinking especially of those who were youth and young adults when President Hinckley gave this powerful, beautiful message.

How old are you (they) now? This talk was given in 1992, so if you were 14 then, you're about 28. If you were 18, you're 32. If you were 22, you're around 36. Now I'm getting into higher math, so I won't go on, but you get the idea. You know who you are.

Do you remember this particular talk? Maybe not, but how are you doing? Do you have little ones? What are you teaching and modeling? Has what President Hinckley said come true in your life? Have you felt the comforting, protecting, guiding influence of ministering angels?

It's not too late—you can still have the marvelous blessings that President Hinckley mentioned.

I want to share another important thought from his talk: "Of course you are peculiar. If the world continues its present trend, and if you walk in obedience to the doctrines and principles of this church, you may become even more peculiar in the eyes of others."

Bring it on!

I love an account of an experience Karl G. Maeser had with a group of missionaries:

> On one occasion, Karl G. Maeser was leading a party of young missionaries across the Alps. As they slowly ascended the steep slope, he looked back and saw a row of sticks thrust into the glacial snow to mark the one safe path across the otherwise

> treacherous mountains. Something about those sticks impressed him, and he halted the company of missionaries and gestured toward the sticks and said, Brethren, there stands the priesthood. They are just common sticks like the rest of us—some of them may even seem to be a little crooked. But the position they hold makes them what they are. If we step aside from the path they mark we are lost! (in Alma P. Burton, *Karl G. Maeser, Mormon Educator* [Salt Lake City: Deseret Book, 1953], 22).

On a beautiful Sunday many years ago I was home watching general conference on TV. President Spencer W. Kimball was speaking in his sweet and distinctive whisper-voice.

There was a knock on the door, and the person who greeted me handed me a pamphlet and asked if I had time to listen to a religious message. I didn't, but as I looked at the pamphlet the person repeated what it had printed on the front: "Hope for ending inflation, sickness, crime, and war."

The fascinating, wonderful thing about the experience was that I could still hear President Kimball's steady, sweet voice in the background, and I knew that HE was the one who could help us figure out how to end inflation, sickness, crime, and war. Plus a whole lot more!

I kept the pamphlet—it reminds me of the difference it makes to have a living prophet to teach and remind us. One thing that makes us peculiar is our knowledge of this fact: There IS a living prophet on the earth!

I used to love to teach this as a missionary. It is so fantastic to teach things that are TRUE. I loved leading up to it with questions like, "Do you think we need a prophet today?" Or, "Do you think God loves us as much as He loved the people in Bible days?" Or perhaps even, "Do you think He still has the power to communicate with His children through a prophet?" And I loved watching the people's response when we would tell them, "There IS a prophet on the earth TODAY. Right now." I could even show them a picture.

Of course, it does us little good to have a living prophet if we don't follow what he says. Think about some of the very specific counsel President Gordon B. Hinckley has given to us. As you read the few excerpts I have chosen to include, ask yourself if it's possible to take his words too literally, or to respond too fully.

On tattoos: "With tattoos, the process is permanent, unless there is another painful and costly undertaking to remove it. Fathers, caution your sons against having their bodies tattooed. They may resist your talk now, but the time will come when they will thank you. A tattoo is graffiti on the temple of the body" ("Great Shall Be the Peace of Thy Children," *Ensign,* November 2000, 50).

Is it possible to take those words too literally? This isn't your mother or your Primary teacher or the librarian at the junior high school—this is a prophet speaking.

(I have to stick in here that the night after I had written the above, I had long dreams about friends of mine who had suddenly showed up with tattoos and piercings. One of them had TWO things in her tongue! Weird!)

On gambling: "We have opposed gambling and liquor and will continue to do so. We regard it as not only our right but our duty to oppose those forces which we feel undermine the moral fiber of society" ("Why We Do Some of the Things We Do," *Ensign,* November 1999, 54).

On debt: "Pay off debt as quickly as you can, and free yourselves from bondage. This is a part of the temporal gospel in which we believe. May the Lord bless you . . . to set your houses in order" ("To the Boys and to the Men," *Ensign,* November 1998, 54).

On pornography: "[Pornography] grows increasingly worse. It is like a raging storm, destroying individuals and families, utterly ruining what was once wholesome and beautiful. I speak of pornography in all of its manifestations . . . sin it is. It is devilish. It is totally inconsistent with the spirit of the gospel, with personal testimony of the things of God" ("A Tragic Evil among Us," *Ensign,* November 2004, 59).

Again, is it possible to take any of these words too literally? Can I say, "Well, he didn't really mean me," or, "He wasn't referring to our home or our family," or, "I'm not really addicted to pornography; I can take it or leave it." Do we even say things like, "That can't be what he meant to say"?

I suppose people may have made similar rationalizations at the time of Moses, Noah, Joseph Smith, and other prophets.

A little crack in the road in the wintertime can end up as a huge pothole as water gets in there and freezes, expanding.

I remember the tiny little fire at the base of Maple Mountain in our town, which eventually burned a huge part of the face of the mountain.

And I think of times when a tiny little infection left unattended can turn into something that no medicine or surgery can repair. It can kill us.

Some things are communicable, and when we indulge in them we're not just putting ourselves in a precarious position but we may be exposing others to harmful things—infections or gambling or pornography or any number of other dangers.

Sometimes I've had chances to choose to follow either the prophet or someone else. If, by following the prophet, I find myself in a minority of earthlings, will I be okay as long as I know I'm standing with God's chosen mouthpiece?

Maybe we don't play poker, and we're not deeply in debt, and we're not indulging in any pornography, but we could still be far away from light and truth and faithfulness in so many other ways.

Maybe someone has cast stones at us, even criticizing us for taking the prophet's words too literally. "Are you going to do every silly little thing he asks you to do?" (We might feel like responding, "Oh, I hope so!")

Read with me from Doctrine and Covenants 107:91–92: "And again, the duty of the President of the office of the High Priesthood is to preside over the whole church, and to be like unto Moses—Behold, here is wisdom; yea, to be a seer, a revelator, a translator, and a prophet, having all the gifts of God which he bestows upon the head of the church."

Our current prophet can do anything that any prophet ever did. If God wants him to and asks him to, he can!

I'm convinced that this part of being peculiar people—this knowledge, this deep assurance that we have of a living prophet—is a critical part of striving to be better when we are already pretty good.

As President Harold B. Lee taught:

> We have some tight places to go before the Lord is through with this church and the world in this dispensation, which is the last dispensation, which shall usher in the coming of the Lord. The gospel was restored to prepare a people ready to receive him. The power of Satan will increase; we see it in evidence on every hand. There will be inroads within the Church. . . . We will see those who profess membership but secretly are plotting and trying to lead people not to follow the leadership that the Lord has set up to preside in this church.
>
> Now the only safety we have as members of this church is to do exactly what the Lord said to the Church in that day when the Church was organized. We must learn to give heed to the words and commandments that the Lord shall give through his prophet, "as he receiveth them, walking in all holiness before me; . . . as if from mine own mouth, in all patience and faith." (D&C 21:4–5.) There will be some things that take patience and faith. You may not like what comes from the authority of the Church. It may contradict your social views. It may interfere

> with some of your social life. But if you listen to these things, as if from the mouth of the Lord himself, with patience and faith, the promise is that "the gates of hell shall not prevail against you; yea, and the Lord God will disperse the powers of darkness from before you, and cause the heavens to shake for your good, and his name's glory." (D&C 21:6) (in Conference Report, October 1970, 152).

Consider, in closing, this counsel and these promises from President Gordon B. Hinckley:

> There is room for improvement in every life. Regardless of our occupations, regardless of our circumstances, we can improve ourselves and while so doing have an effect on the lives of those about us. . . .
>
> We can lower our voices a few decibels. We can return good for evil. We can smile when anger might be so much easier. We can exercise self-control and self-discipline and dismiss any affront levied against us.
>
> Let us be a happy people. The Lord's plan is a plan of happiness. The way will be lighter, the worries will be fewer, the confrontations will be less difficult if we cultivate a spirit of happiness.
>
> . . . May a spirit of peace and love attend you wherever you may be. May there be harmony in your lives. . . . May you kneel in prayer before the Almighty with thanksgiving unto Him for His bounteous

blessings ("Each a Better Person," *Ensign*, November 2002, 99).

Follow the prophet!

HIGHLY RECOMMENDED READING

Any talk or article or book by President Gordon B. Hinckley.

Gordon B. Hinckley, "A Chosen Generation," *Ensign*, May 1992, 69–71.

Gordon B. Hinckley, "Each a Better Person," *Ensign*, November 2002, 99.

Spencer W. Kimball, *The Miracle of Forgiveness*, Salt Lake City: Bookcraft, 1969.

Ezra Taft Benson, "Beware of Pride," *Ensign*, May 1989, 4–7.

Howard W. Hunter, "Follow the Son of God," *Ensign*, November 1994, 87–88.

CHAPTER 13

What Lack I Yet?

In the New Testament, the story is told of a rich young man who asked the Savior what good thing he could do to have eternal life. The Savior responded that the young man should keep the commandments. Interestingly, the young man responded by asking which ones. "Name one," we can almost imagine him saying.

So Jesus again shared some of the commandments, including honoring father and mother, loving our neighbors, and that we should not murder, steal, or commit adultery.

The young ruler must have felt very encouraged, because he said he had done all these things since he was a boy.

And then he asked Jesus the magic question: "What lack I yet?"

This is the way Jesus responded: "If thou wilt be perfect, go and sell that thou hast, and give to the poor, and thou shalt have treasure in heaven: and come and follow me."

Oh, my—the Savior asked the young ruler if he wanted to be whole!

Well, the one thing the young man lacked was the one thing he could not do, even for a promise of eternal life (including treasures in heaven). He apparently had lots of stuff, lots of possessions, and he just couldn't part with them (see Matthew 19:16–22).

The young ruler's experience may come close to the essence of striving to be better when we're already pretty good—honestly asking, "What lack I yet?" This is a very sobering, serious question, because if I ask with real intent, I'm going to receive an answer. How will I respond?

It has been my experience that there are two questions I've asked in particular that have brought some very interesting answers. These two questions are similar to but slightly different from "what lack I yet?" They are:

"Heavenly Father, is there anything I'm doing that isn't right for me?" To me this one deals with commission—what do I need to STOP doing.

"Heavenly Father, is there anything I'm not doing that I need to be doing?" This question, of course, deals with omission—what do I need to START doing.

I may not ask these questions every day, but even when I don't ask "out loud," I still receive whispered answers to both.

Do you ever feel overwhelmed by such things? When you ask such questions of your Heavenly Father, does it seem like a never-ending list pops into your mind, both of things you should stop doing and things you need to start doing?

I don't want to beat up on anyone. I don't want to add fuel to any discouragement fire, or dig someone's screaming pit any deeper. I'm convinced that for most of us there is quite enough guilt in our lives. We've already had enough of feeling overwhelmed, inadequate, and even hopeless at times.

I feel deeply about all that I've shared, but I also feel that we're sometimes out of balance. We want to be better, but we keep thinking that we've heard or read, "Be ye therefore perfect by this afternoon," or "I will go and do all that God has commanded all at once."

Without turning away from the realization that life IS hard, and it IS a test, and there IS the need to eventually become perfect (whole, complete, and pure), I want to encourage you to stop for a "take a deep breath" moment. Whoa! Relax! Be still! Enjoy this amazing, complex, sometimes frustrating journey!

I don't know what it is about us that causes us to think so much more often of the mistakes we've made than the things we've done right, but in my experience it's too true that we do. Why is it so difficult to focus on our strengths, on our good actions, on how much we HAVE done instead of how much we haven't done?

Ask yourself, "What are some of my mistakes and weaknesses?" and you'll probably have a long list lickety-split.

But ask yourself, "What are my strengths; what good things have I done in the world today?" and it's often a struggle. Maybe we feel it smacks of pride to allow "well done" to enter our minds and hearts.

Please don't let anything I've shared in this book cause you to add to your list of "things I've not done," or "things I'll probably never be able to do," or "stuff that's going to keep me out of Heaven," or "why God is mad at me." Quit it!

What I feel as deeply as anything I've shared is that we talk back too much—to our Heavenly Father. Yes, we do. Think about it. How many times have you kept Him from telling you how wonderful you are and how much He loves you? I really mean it—I want you to think about that and see if I'm right. He'll tell you "good job" and you'll jump in and talk back, telling Him, "oh, I should have . . ." or "but I didn't . . ." I say again, quit it! Let Him love you! Let Heavenly Father and Jesus Christ put their arms around you and assure you that you're going in the right direction, and that They understand it's not always easy. Please!

I'd like to share in this context a personal experience that I've related before. When I was first a missionary, I went as far from home as I could go without starting back. It was about 10,000 miles from Utah to Hong Kong. After spending a few days with President and Sister Taylor at the mission headquarters, I was assigned to Taiwan, a zone of the Southern Far East Mission.

I arrived not knowing any Mandarin. I had spent a week in the Missionary Home in Salt Lake City, but although that was a fantastic experience, there was no language instruction.

Mandarin did not sound like a language to me. It was like little bursts of noise, and each noise had a tone, and it was all so new and strange to my ear. It was as if the people, including little children (who would really show off!), were singing a strange, unrecognizable song.

Slowly but surely I began to learn how to get the right tone on some of these "noises." Like many other missionaries, I unconsciously nodded or bobbed my head to try to emphasize which tone I meant. If you saw a video of those early efforts, I think you would laugh. Or cry.

Gradually I could say hello to people and understand a smattering of words. I even learned a little song from the children, only to learn later that I was singing I was a monkey, swinging from trees and eating bananas. Oh well . . . it seemed to entertain them.

One of the first long things we were to learn was how to tell of Joseph Smith's experience in the spring of 1820. Each morning, my companion, Jan Bair, and I would ride our bikes to the outskirts of Tainan and she would help me go over and over this "Joseph Smith Story," memorizing and improving it little by little.

And then one day she said, "You're ready." Oh! I actually didn't want to be ready! It meant she expected me to share it with someone!

I admit it was hard not to pray that no one would let us in their home on that beautiful day in November. And it was hard not to pray that even if someone answered the door, they'd tell us to go away.

Eventually we were in the home of Sister Lin, and she wanted us to teach her. Sister Bair began, and I did my best to put the right Chinese words on the flannel board (THERE'S an indication of how long ago this was—it was 1962). I couldn't read any of the words on the flannel strips, but I had written on the back what went where, and when. I even had arrows so I wouldn't get them upside down.

At some point it became very quiet in Sister Lin's small living room, and Sister Bair was smiling at me. It was time.

In that terrifying instant, a realization came into my heart. At that moment in my life, all I could do was the best I could do.

And so I began to say my little noises the best I could, likely bobbing my head around ever so slightly as I went along.

Here was the miracle: the Holy Ghost was able to take my little noises over to Sister Lin, and as they entered her ears, her mind, and her heart, she heard: *A young boy named Joseph Smith went to a grove of trees to pray, and the Father and the Son appeared to him . . .*

Can you imagine my feelings? Can you imagine the joy and wonder of it! All I could do was the best I could do, and *that was what He was asking.*

Let me see if I can explain even more deeply the important lesson I learned as a very new, very young missionary far away from home: Heavenly Father was asking for my best. He wasn't asking me to do more than I could. But He also wasn't asking me to do less. He knew my situation. He knew what I could do, and He knew what I couldn't do.

President Hinckley helped me understand this when he said: "Please don't nag yourself with thoughts of failure. Do not set goals far beyond your capacity to achieve. Simply do what you can do, in the best way you know, and the Lord will accept of your effort" ("Rise to the Stature of the Divine within You," *Ensign*, November 1989, 96).

Part of what I learned is that too often I don't include Them (my Heavenly Father, the Savior, and the Holy Ghost) in my deliberations and decisions. I may think, "I can't do that!" Too often I don't add something like this: "I can't do that without Heavenly help."

Emma Lou Thayne gave us a wonderful phrase in her hymn "Where Can I Turn for Peace?" (*Hymns*, no. 129): "reaches my reaching." Yes! We do the best we can do—we do all we can do—and They reach our reaching.

That was exactly what happened in a small home in the south of Taiwan as I did the best I could to teach Sister Lin about Joseph Smith's experience. Heavenly help came to reach my reaching, to help me share and to help Sister Lin understand.

Part of what I want you to know about the experience is that it was a very frightening, challenging moment for me, and at the same time it turned into one of the best, sweetest, and most important learning experiences of my entire mission. He meant what He said! He really DID send Heavenly help! But first I had to "go to the edge"—I had to do something that I wasn't sure I could do. I had to realize that it was true—that without Their help, the sweet miracle couldn't have happened.

I am convinced that we will never be asked to do things we cannot do. When we ask, "What lack I yet?" and when we strive to be better when we're already pretty good, I pray we will be conscious of the fact that without Heavenly help we'd likely be right to say, "It's too much . . . I can't do it . . . I'll never make it."

But with God, NOTHING is too hard. NOTHING IS IMPOSSIBLE! (see Luke 1:37; Genesis 18:14).

"Arise therefore, and be doing, and the Lord be with thee" (1 Chronicles 22:16).

And so He DOES ask us to be perfect. Through His prophet President Gordon B. Hinckley He DID ask us to try a little harder to be a little better.

President Hinckley also said this, which has helped me in so many ways: "We are far from being a perfect society as we travel along the road to immortality and eternal life. The great work of the Church in furthering this process is to help men and women to move toward the perfection exemplified by the Savior of mankind. We are not likely to reach that goal in a day or a year or a lifetime. But as we strive in this direction, we shall become better men and women, sons and daughters of God" ("150-Year Drama: A Personal View of Our History," *Ensign*, April 1980, 14).

Perfection is POSSIBLE, but perfection is a PROCESS. I had an "aha" moment when I was studying some things Hugh W. Nibley had said about perfection. Here is the part that grabbed my attention: "You can be perfect in certain things, but that means *perpetual repentance*. Notice, this is an ongoing process, to be perfect. He doesn't expect you to achieve that all the way. As Brigham Young used to tell the Saints, 'Learn everything.' Okay, I'll go home and learn everything. No, you won't—he knew you wouldn't. But if that wasn't the goal, you wouldn't learn very much. That's the point. And if you're not striving to be perfect, you won't repent" (*Teachings of the Book of Mormon—Semester 1: Transcripts of Lectures Presented to an Honors Book of Mormon Class at Brigham Young University,*

1988–1990 [Provo: Foundation for Ancient Research and Mormon Studies], 93).

Oh, that speaks to me! Especially the last part: "If you're not striving to be perfect, you won't repent." No wonder "what lack I yet?" is such an incredible question! The process of striving to be better when you're already pretty good is a process of repenting, changing, reaching . . . and knowing that God is with you in every moment.

Listen to these words from the hymn "Zion Stands with Hills Surrounded" (*Hymns*, no. 43):

> *In the furnace God may prove thee,*
> *Thence to bring thee forth more bright,*
> *But can never cease to love thee;*
> *Thou art precious in his sight.*
> *God is with thee, God is with thee;*
> *Thou shalt triumph in his might.*

Isn't that an encouraging message? God is with us, and in HIS might we will triumph!

Years ago I was wandering around in my studying and came across a quote from President Brigham Young that brought such comfort to me, and then suddenly yanked me back a bit. First I'll share the comforting part:

> It may appear strange to some of you, and it certainly does to the world, to say it is possible for a man or woman to become perfect on this earth. It is

> written "Be ye therefore perfect, even as your Father which is in heaven is perfect. . . ."
>
> If the first passage I have quoted is not worded to our understanding, we can alter the phraseology of the sentence, and say, "Be ye as perfect as ye can," for that is all we can do, though it is written, be ye perfect as your Father who is in heaven is perfect.
>
> To be as perfect as we possibly can, according to our knowledge, is to be just as perfect as our Father in heaven is. He cannot be any more perfect than He knows how, any more than we.
>
> When we are doing as well as we know how in the sphere and station which we occupy here, we are justified in the justice, righteousness, mercy, and judgment that go before the Lord of heaven and earth. We are as justified as the angels who are before the throne of God.

As I said, up to that point I had felt comforted, understood, pretty good. And then came the last part of the quote:

> The sin that will cleave to all the posterity of Adam and Eve is, that they have not done as well as they knew how (in *Journal of Discourses,* 26 vols. [London: Latter-day Saints' Book Depot, 1854–1886], 2:129–30).

I think you can now understand that although the first part was very comforting, the last sentence reminded me I need to be "up and doing," striving.

It's as the Apostle Paul stated: "For that which I do I allow not: for what I would, that do I not; but what I hate, that do I" (Romans 7:15). And also "For the good that I would I do not: but the evil which I would not, that I do" (Romans 7:19).

Still, President James E. Faust reminds us of God's love and understanding: "All of us have made wrong turns along the way. I believe the kind and merciful God, whose children we are, will judge us as lightly as He can for the wrongs that we have done and give us the maximum blessing for the good that we do" ("Woman, Why Weepest Thou?" *Ensign,* November 1996, 53).

I know the principles of the gospel can save me, purify me, and change my heart. I love to sing not just "Teach me all that I must know," or "Teach me all that I must do," but "Teach me all that I must BE to live with Him someday." I want to be comfortable in Heaven, to feel a sense of belonging. I hope I can be peculiar enough to live in a Zion society, happy to be one heart and one mind with everyone, happy with equality, happy with doing my best, happy with the thought that there are no poor among us.

The key to having this peculiar happiness is found in the gospel of Jesus Christ. It is found in LIGHT and TRUTH. It is found in striving to be better when you're already pretty good.

It is found in knowing that the gospel of "Be ye therefore perfect" is also the gospel of "here a little and there a little," line upon line, precept upon precept, and don't run faster than you have strength. It's knowing that what Heavenly Father asks is for us to do the best we can. He inspired His living prophet to tell us: Try a little harder to be a little better.

So here we are, dear friends, living our uncommon lives,

sometimes hearing the snickering and noticing the finger-pointing coming from GAS (remember, this is an acronym for "great and spacious") locations all around, and perhaps encountering the word that others use with the thought that they're putting us down: "You people are so PECULIAR!"

Yes, we are. It's true. We like it that way. We want it that way. We're going to continue striving to be better.

We believe we have been sent to this earth to begin a journey back to our Heavenly Home, and we believe that as children of God we are known and loved, and that He has a plan for each of us, individually, to help us return.

Among many other things, we'll continue to pray, study the scriptures, attend meetings, partake of the sacrament, pay an honest tithing, hold family home evening and family council, participate in temple worship, and keep the Sabbath day holy.

We're going to fast and contribute generous fast offerings, bear each other's burdens, accept callings and serve without financial recompense, work on preparedness, make and keep covenants, be clean, serve others, seek to be genuinely humble, keep the Word of Wisdom, follow the prophet, and show reverence for the name of God.

We will continue to read the Book of Mormon and other scriptures and good books. (By the way, wasn't it a magnificent experience to read with each other during the last few months of 2005? I feel so thankful that President Hinckley asked us to do that. Everywhere I went I would ask, "How's your 'assignment' coming?" There were some great responses! Didn't we see each other reading in all kinds of interesting circumstances?)

We will continue to mourn with those who mourn, be honest in our relationships and business dealings, serve missions, live worthy of the companionship of the Holy Ghost, do our best in nurturing children, honor our parents, do sacred work in temples for our ancestors, and gather their histories.

We will contribute to humanitarian efforts as well as temple building and the Perpetual Education Fund, comfort those who stand in need of comfort, strive to be free from debt, work to strengthen individuals and families, be good examples of righteousness and neighborliness, and seek after that which is virtuous, lovely, of good report, and praiseworthy.

We will continue to be happy, to press forward with a steadfastness in Christ and a brightness of hope—with JOY! I've been convinced for a long, long time that we ought to be the happiest people anywhere.

President Gordon B. Hinckley has said: "I see a wonderful future in a very uncertain world. . . . If we will simply live the gospel, we will be blessed in a magnificent and wonderful way. We will be looked upon as a peculiar people who have found the key to a peculiar happiness" ("Look to the Future," *Ensign*, November 1997, 69).

We are not ashamed of our membership in the Church or the gospel of Jesus Christ, because we know it is the power of God unto salvation (see Romans 1:16). It's a good way to live. It's a WONDERFUL way to live. Every single thing we are asked to do is tied to unbelievable opportunities and blessings, to joy and peace. We know that we cannot even comprehend the things God has prepared for those who love Him and serve Him (see 1 Corinthians 2:9).

We will endure through our deep waters and fiery trials (see *Hymns,* no. 85) with patience and faith and good cheer, knowing that we are not alone (see D&C 68:6).

We want to do what Jesus would do, and we want to be what He wants us to be. "I'll go where you want me to go, I'll do what you want me to do, I'll say what you want me to say, I'll be what you want me to be" (*Hymns,* no. 270).

We will continue to be grateful and to express our gratitude.

And in our own peculiar, sacred ways, we will stand as witnesses of God and Jesus Christ at all times and in all things, and in all places we may be in, even until death, that we may be redeemed of God and be numbered with those of the first resurrection, that we may have eternal life (see Mosiah 18:8–11).

This is the desire of our hearts.

HIGHLY RECOMMENDED READING

Patricia T. Holland, " 'One Thing Needful': Becoming Women of Greater Faith in Christ," *Ensign,* October 1987, 26–33.

Jeffrey R. Holland, "He Hath Filled the Hungry with Good Things," *Ensign,* November 1997, 64–66.

James E. Faust, "That We Might Know Thee," *Ensign,* January 1999, 2–5.

Robert Millet, *Are We There Yet?* Salt Lake City: Deseret Book, 2005.

Russell M. Nelson, "Perfection Pending," *Ensign,* November 1995, 86–88.

Web Sharing

We're going to try something peculiar (oh, really?) in connection with this little book. We're going to have a place on the Deseret Book web site where we can talk to each other about our ideas and adventures in striving to be better.

The location will be DeseretBook.com, then click on Time Out for Women, and then click on Message Board.

The thread will be called "PECULIARPEOPLE." It will start as soon as the book is published and will run for as long as there is interest.

This will give a chance for interaction with other readers and also with some of the "Arrowheads," including MEE. The Arrowheads are a group with which I meet every so often to gather ideas, refine thoughts, and share inspiration. They've been kind and generous with their time, friendship, and feedback.

We particularly had a great time with "The Order of the Arrow" (see chapter 3 in this book) and thus came the name of our group: Arrowheads.

Each Arrowhead who joins the online discussion will be distinguished by "Arrow" at the beginning of the user name. For example, my user name is ArrowMEE (big surprise). Others will have names such as ArrowLWA, ArrowBELL, and ArrowCush. We're not doing this because we think our ideas will be the best or our responses the most witty and wise, but just so you'll know when you're "talking" to one of the Arrowheads.

Please join us!